CONFERENCE PROCEEDINGS

Directors as Guardians of Compliance and Ethics Within the Corporate Citadel

What the Policy Community Should Know

Michael D. Greenberg

RAND Center for Corporate Ethics and Governance
A RAND INSTITUTE FOR CIVIL JUSTICE CENTER

This report was funded with pooled resources from the RAND Center for Corporate Ethics and Governance, with additional support provided by Bridgeway. This research was conducted within the RAND Center for Corporate Ethics and Governance, which is part of the RAND Institute for Civil Justice, a unit of the RAND Corporation.

Library of Congress Cataloging-in-Publication Data

Directors as guardians of compliance and ethics within the corporate citadel : what the policy community should know / Michael D. Greenberg.

p. cm.

Includes bibliographical references.

ISBN 978-0-8330-5032-8 (pbk. : alk. paper)

1. Corporations—Corrupt practices—United States—Congresses. 2. Corporate governance—Moral and ethical aspects—United States—Congresses. 3. Business ethics—United States—Congresses. I. Greenberg, Michael D., 1969-

HV6769.D57 2010

658.1'2—dc22

2010027677

Cover image courtesy of Terry Vine/Blend Images/Getty Images

Published 2010 by the RAND Corporation
1776 Main Street, P.O. Box 2138, Santa Monica, CA 90407-2138
1200 South Hayes Street, Arlington, VA 22202-5050
4570 Fifth Avenue, Suite 600, Pittsburgh, PA 15213-2665
RAND URL: http://www.rand.org/
To order RAND documents or to obtain additional information, contact
Distribution Services: Telephone: (310) 451-7002;
Fax: (310) 451-6915; Email: order@rand.org

PREFACE

The collapse of financial markets in late 2008 has invited renewed questions about the governance, compliance, and ethics practices of firms throughout the U.S. and global economies. On May 12, 2010, RAND convened a symposium in Washington, D.C., on the perspective and role of corporate boards of directors in overseeing ethics and compliance matters within their firms. Participants included thought leaders from the ranks of public company directors at major corporations, together with business executives, ethics and compliance officers, and stakeholders from the nonprofit sector, academia, and government. Discussions focused on the challenges that directors face in this rapidly evolving role; on the responsibility of boards to oversee corporate cultures that foster integrity and compliance with the law; and on steps that business leaders and policymakers might take to better encourage and empower directors in their oversight and, by extension, to strengthen compliance mechanisms and ethical leadership within firms.

These RAND conference proceedings summarize key issues and topics from the May 12, 2010, symposium. The document is not intended to be a transcript; instead it is organized by the major themes of discussion, pointing out areas of agreement as well as disagreement. With the exception of three invited papers that were written in advance and presented by symposium participants, we do not attribute remarks to specific persons.

This report was funded with pooled resources from the RAND Center for Corporate Ethics and Governance, with additional support provided by Bridgeway. These proceedings should be of interest to policymakers, regulators, corporate directors and executives, compliance and ethics practitioners, shareholders, and other stakeholders with interests in corporate governance, ethics, and compliance practice issues, both in the United States and abroad.

THE RAND CENTER FOR CORPORATE ETHICS AND GOVERNANCE

The RAND Center for Corporate Ethics and Governance is committed to improving public understanding of corporate ethics, law, and governance, and to identifying specific ways that businesses can operate ethically, legally, and profitably at the same time. The center's work is supported by voluntary contributions from private-sector organizations and individuals with interests in research on these topics.

The center is part of the RAND Institute for Civil Justice (ICJ), whose mission is to improve private and public decisionmaking on civil legal issues by supplying policymakers with the results of objective, empirically based, analytic research. ICJ facilitates change in the civil justice system by analyzing trends and outcomes, identifying and evaluating policy options, and bringing together representatives of different interests to debate alternative solutions to policy problems. ICJ builds on a long tradition of RAND research characterized by an interdisciplinary, empirical approach to public policy issues and by rigorous standards of quality, objectivity, and independence.

ICJ research is supported by pooled grants from corporations, trade and professional associations, and individuals; by government grants and contracts; and by private foundations. ICJ disseminates its work widely to the legal, business, and research communities and to the general public. In accordance with RAND policy, all ICJ research products are subject to peer review before publication. ICJ publications do not necessarily reflect the opinions or policies of the research sponsors or of the ICJ Board of Overseers.

Information about ICJ is available online (http://www.rand.org/icj/). Inquiries about research projects should be directed to

James Dertouzos, Director
RAND Institute for Civil Justice
1776 Main Street
P.O. Box 2138
Santa Monica, CA 90407–2138
310-393–0411 x7476
Fax: 310-451-6979
James_Dertouzos@rand.org

Information about ICJ's Center for Corporate Ethics and Governance is also available online (http://www.rand.org/icj/centers/corporate_ethics/). Inquiries about the center and questions or comments specific to this document should be directed to

Michael Greenberg, Director
RAND Center for Corporate Ethics and Governance
4570 Fifth Avenue, Suite 600
Pittsburgh, PA 15213-2665
412-683-2300 x4648
Fax: 412-683-2800
Michael_Greenberg@rand.org

CONTENTS

Preface iii
Summary vii
Acknowledgments xi
Abbreviations xiii
1. Introduction 1
2. Invited Remarks from Symposium Participants 5
3. Challenges and Opportunities for Boards in Performing the Ethics and Compliance Oversight Role 13
The First C&E Commandment for Directors: Know Thy Company 14
Ensuring Ethical Culture Is a Top Responsibility for Directors and Feeds into Other Aspects of Their Role 15
For Directors, the Ability to See into C&E Matters Within the Firm Is Limited and Demands Putting Appropriate Mechanisms in Place 16
Although Applying Ethics to Business Strategy Decisions Can Sometimes Be Ambiguous, Boards Can Nevertheless Take Concrete Steps to Improve C&E Performance in Firms 17
It Can Be Difficult to Mandate Ethical Behavior Through the Law, but the Federal Sentencing Guidelines Offer Critical Guidance to Boards 18
4. Empowerment, Resources, and Policy: How Do We Set Directors Up to Succeed in Ethics and Compliance Oversight? 19
The Federal Sentencing Guidelines Have Created More Oversight Responsibility and Liability Risk for Directors, So More Robust, Targeted Board Education on C&E Is Needed 20
Fiduciary Duty Calls for a Robust Decisionmaking Process on C&E 21
Empowering the CECO Is a Path to Empowering the Board 22
More Specific Feedback from Regulators, Citing Cases in Which Companies Benefited from Specific, Strong C&E Program Steps, Would Drive More-Effective Corporate Programs 23
The Conversation Between Directors and the CECO Is a Key Asset for the Board 25
Appendix A: Symposium Participants 27
Appendix B: Symposium Agenda 29
Appendix C: Invited Papers from Panel Participants 31
Evolving Role and Liability of the Board of Directors for Ethics and Compliance Oversight 31
Corporate Counsel Perspective: The Crisis of Ethics and the Need for a Compliance-Savvy Board 41
Board Oversight of Compliance, Ethics, Integrity, and Reputation Risks: What Directors Need to Know 50
Appendix D: Twenty Questions That Boards of Directors Should Ask About Compliance and Ethics 57
References 59

SUMMARY

Advancing corporate ethics, compliance, and governance has been a significant policy priority for the U.S. government for at least 20 years, going back to the 1991 promulgation of the Federal Sentencing Guidelines for Organizations (FSG). This concern has achieved new prominence in the wake of the financial collapse of 2008, and policymakers have once again become focused on corporate compliance and ethics (C&E) programs and on the oversight role of corporate boards as potential avenues for preventing excesses and scandals in the private sector. In principle, the institutional mechanisms of boards and C&E programs should have helped to protect firms from excessive risk-taking and opportunistic misconduct. But in practice, at least in some financial services firms in the lead-up to the collapse, they did not. It remains to be seen whether history will view the Great Recession as accruing, in significant part, to lapses in corporate ethics and governance practices. But in the wake of the financial collapse, policymakers and business leaders alike have been galvanized to reconsider the responsibility of boards for C&E oversight and the notion that ethics, compliance, and risk management may be fundamental to the role of corporate directors. Basic notions about the fiduciary duty of directors, and about the protection of shareholder and societal interests, are consequently evolving rapidly.

It is in this context that RAND convened a May 12, 2010, symposium titled "Directors as the Guardians of Ethics and Compliance Within the Corporate Citadel: What the Policy Community Needs to Know." The purpose of the symposium was to stimulate a broad conversation about the role of directors in providing C&E oversight in U.S. corporations. The symposium brought together more than two dozen persons, some with distinguished service as directors on leading public company boards, and others with long experience serving as ethics and compliance officers within firms. Participants also included stakeholders and thought leaders with backgrounds in the non-profit sector and in government. Discussions at the conference focused on (1) challenges and opportunities for boards in performing a C&E oversight role and (2) resources and policy that might assist directors in strengthening the C&E function and in more effectively carrying out oversight responsibility.

Several major themes emerged from the symposium discussions. The first was that corporate directors do have basic responsibilities for monitoring ethics and compliance in their firms and infusing related values into their decisionmaking, but that these responsibilities are broadly hampered by a lack of training and awareness on the part of many outside directors. More robust, targeted efforts to educate directors on this aspect of board responsibility, and on ways to carry out the responsibility effectively, are needed. A second major theme was that a primary responsibility of directors involves gathering the information they need to really understand their firms, as well as related risks, strategies, and operational concerns. This data-gathering obligation takes many different forms, but with regard to C&E, it means that directors need to gather information both about their firms' "ethical culture" and, more concretely, about

C&E processes, initiatives, gaps, challenges, and performance. A third theme discussed at length in the symposium was that directors are not operating in a vacuum when it comes to carrying out their responsibility for C&E oversight. They have an agent in the person who carries day-to-day responsibility for overseeing a firm's C&E program: the chief ethics and compliance officer, or CECO. The CECO provides a major conduit of information on C&E matters back to the board. When properly positioned and empowered, the CECO can become a key resource for the board in fulfilling its own mandates to monitor and ensure the effectiveness of C&E practice within the firm.

INVITED REMARKS FROM THREE PANELISTS

The initial session of the symposium was dedicated to invited remarks from three panelists, all with expertise in the governance obligations of boards and the C&E function within firms. The first panelist discussed directors' evolving role and liability in C&E oversight, and the reality that directors face significant civil liability risk in connection with state law fiduciary duty and shifting stakeholder and regulatory expectations. The second panelist focused on the in-house counsel perspective and the need for a compliance-savvy board. He suggested that many corporate C&E programs are vulnerable to being treated as "check-the-box" exercises rather than as fundamental commitments to accountability and ethical leadership within their organizations. In this regard, he suggested that the board has a central role to play and must become knowledgeable about C&E matters if it is to adequately discharge its responsibilities. The third panelist discussed how the CECO occupies a pivotal position in empowering the board, driving an effective C&E program, and making ethical culture into a reality within the firm. He suggested that the expansion of board C&E responsibilities has only made the CECO role more important as a resource, that board involvement is simultaneously crucial to empowering the CECO, and that the CECO's function is likewise crucial to empowering and informing the board.

CHALLENGES AND OPPORTUNITIES FOR BOARDS IN PERFORMING THE C&E OVERSIGHT ROLE

The second session of the symposium involved a moderated discussion on challenges, issues, and opportunities for directors in connection with C&E monitoring and oversight. Participants addressed a broad range of related concerns. The session opened with reflections on the need for directors to balance C&E as an important issue on their radar, but as only one among the many specific demands now being placed on directors' time. It was observed that directors have oversight obligations in many areas — legal, information technology (IT), risk, audit, strategy, Sarbanes-Oxley Act of 2002 (SOX) Section 404 compliance, and obligations under new Securities and Exchange Commission (SEC) disclosure rules — all of which represent competing demands, in addition to their more basic responsibilities concerning review of company performance and protection of shareholder rights. For independent directors who are unlikely to spend more than several weeks a year carrying out their duties, the simple press of time was identified as a significant challenge with regard to both C&E and these various other aspects of oversight. Efficiency and effectiveness were therefore stressed as important aims for directors in husbanding their time and making the strongest possible contribution on C&E.

In a different vein, the opening remarks for the session underlined that in carrying out their responsibilities, directors help to set the ethical "tone at the top" of their organizations. This basic aspect of what directors do in contributing to organizational culture was identified as pivotal to their role.

Some of the discussions touched on defining the essence of the C&E oversight role for directors, on the ways that directors can better inform themselves about C&E matters within the firm, and on the appropriateness and effectiveness of outside legal mandates for board involvement in C&E. The reality that the problems of corporate misbehavior and ethically dubious conduct remain abundant in the United States despite widespread awareness of their existence among directors was a major theme of conversation, with a serial focus on several potential root causes. Session participants generally agreed on several points:

- The first C&E commandment for directors is "Know Thy Company."
- Ensuring ethical culture is a top responsibility for directors and feeds into other aspects of the director role.
- Because the ability of directors to see into C&E matters within the firm is limited, appropriate management mechanisms must be put into place.
- Although applying ethics to business strategy decisions can sometimes be ambiguous, there are concrete steps that boards can take to improve C&E performance in firms.
- It can be difficult to mandate ethical behavior through the law, but the FSG nevertheless offer critical guidance to boards.

EMPOWERMENT, RESOURCES, AND POLICY — HOW DO WE SET DIRECTORS UP TO SUCCEED IN C&E OVERSIGHT?

Participants in the final session of the symposium focused more deeply on the topics of board empowerment and policy, and on ways to help and encourage directors to play a stronger and more meaningful independent C&E oversight role, as opposed to simply "rubber-stamping" management reports. One part of the discussion touched on government enforcement authority and liability risk pertaining to C&E matters, and the incentives these policies create for persons serving as directors. The reality was underscored that boards face heightened civil liability on C&E, resulting from a combination of recent legal and regulatory developments. It was also observed that there is serious interest in the regulatory community in facilitating board engagement in C&E oversight, as well as concern that some boards and directors are not adequately scrutinizing these issues. The question was raised, How can the policy community help in promoting stronger recognition of C&E issues in the director community, and better related performance by boards and by management? Some pragmatic steps along these lines, such as director certifications in C&E or bringing people with C&E backgrounds onto boards as outside directors, were discussed. Another topic of discussion involved specific steps that managers and CECOs can take in building stronger C&E programs within firms. It was noted that although these kinds of programmatic steps are somewhat removed from the immediate role of directors, more robust, targeted education for directors, together with a basic familiarity with the elements of a strong C&E program, can help directors to ask the right questions of their CECOs and to confirm that appropriate controls and institutional mechanisms are put in place.

Several of the major points of discussion and agreement during the session included the following:

- The FSG have created more oversight responsibility and liability risk for directors, so there is a need for more robust, targeted board education on C&E.
- Fiduciary duty calls for a robust decisionmaking process on C&E.
- Empowering the CECO is a path to empowering the board.
- Boards should seek out multiple sources of information and reporting on C&E.
- More specific feedback from regulators, citing cases in which companies benefited from specific, strong C&E program steps, would drive more-effective corporate programs.
- The "conversation" between directors and the CECO is a key asset for the board.

ACKNOWLEDGMENTS

I wish to thank the panelists, speakers, and all those who engaged in the symposium discussions, without whom the exchange of ideas documented here would not have been possible. I would particularly like to thank the current and former directors who participated in the conference, including Lovida Coleman, Roxanne Decyk, Ann Korologos, George Muñoz, Shirley Peterson, and Larry Zicklin. I would also like to thank the authors of the invited white papers and others who spoke at the symposium, including Gary Brown, Jack Hansen, and Keith Darcy, as well as J. Troy Beatty of the Securities and Exchange Commission and Peter Gleason of the National Association of Corporate Directors. Acting as my symposium co-chair, Donna Boehme provided invaluable contributions in structuring the discussions on May 12, and in bringing the right group of people to the conference table. Preparation of this symposium proceedings report was facilitated by generous support from Bridgeway.

Finally, I would like to thank Amy Coombe, Michelle Horner, and Jamie Morikawa from RAND for their assistance in every aspect of putting the conference together, managing logistics, capturing the discussions on the day of the event, and generating this proceedings document. *Per aspera ad astra.*

ABBREVIATIONS

ACC	Association of Corporate Counsel
C&E	compliance and ethics
CECO	chief ethics and compliance officer
CEO	chief executive officer
CFO	chief financial officer
CIA	corporate integrity agreement
DOJ	U.S. Department of Justice
DPA	deferred prosecution agreement
ERM	enterprise risk management
FSG	Federal Sentencing Guidelines for Organizations
ICJ	RAND Institute for Civil Justice
IT	information technology
NACD	National Association of Corporate Directors
SEC	Securities and Exchange Commission
SOX	Sarbanes-Oxley Act of 2002
USSC	United States Sentencing Commission

1. INTRODUCTION

The role of boards and directors in corporate oversight appears to be in the midst of change. The financial collapse of 2008 and the Great Recession that began thereafter have spurred public sentiment that inadequate controls, faulty organizational cultures, poor risk management practice, and lapses in governance all contributed in some way in the lead-up to the crisis. Many commentators have observed that the compliance and ethics (C&E) function within firms, which should have helped to protect large financial services companies from excessive risk-taking and (in some instances) dishonest practice, failed spectacularly. Of course, the eventual cascade of financial risk across institutions extended beyond the responsibility or influence of any single organization to mitigate. Nevertheless, the fact that many organizations undertook poorly understood risks in pursuit of unsustainable short-term gains, with only very limited transparency to senior executives and board oversight, suggests that basic aspects of organizational culture and controls failed to perform as expected by stakeholders. Some would view these shortcomings as a confirmation that C&E programs in too many firms are in fact nothing more than "check-the-box" exercises — i.e., they fulfill legal requirements specified on paper but do not effect fundamental change in corporate behavior. And of course, the shortcomings also invite the question, Where were the ultimate guardians of shareholder value in all of this? Where were the boards of directors when we needed them most?

Interestingly, even before the financial crisis broke in 2008, there was significant judicial and regulatory movement toward increased responsibility for directors in overseeing the C&E function within firms. That responsibility arose from the *Caremark* and *Stone v. Ritter* precedents,[1] which established that the fiduciary duty of directors embraces an obligation to monitor compliance as an aspect of firm management and, moreover, to implement internal programs to detect potential violations of law and corporate policy. The failure of boards to act in this way places directors at personal risk for civil liability under state law. In addition, relevant guidance on director oversight for C&E has been provided, in part, by the Federal Sentencing Guidelines for Organizations (FSG). The FSG speak at length to the parameters for an effective corporate C&E program. And just as the failure to establish effective programs pursuant to the FSG places organizations at increased risk when violations of law occur, so too does it place directors at increased risk under the civil liability framework established by *Caremark* and *Stone*. Further standards for what corporate C&E programs need to look like have emerged from other sources of authority as well, such as U.S. Department of Justice (DOJ) memoranda outlining factors considered in prosecutorial discretion, and major illustrative deferred prosecution agreements (DPAs) entered into by public companies. Taken together, these various legal authorities suggest substantial new responsibilities for boards in setting up

---

[1] See *In re Caremark International Inc. Derivative Litigation*, 1996; and *Stone v. Ritter*, 2006.

and overseeing the institutional framework to prevent and mitigate the occurrence of opportunistic misconduct.

In light of the shifting parameters of director responsibility in this area, it remains far from clear whether boards truly understand their legal obligations on C&E, much less whether they have the information and resources needed to carry out those obligations effectively. With regard to the former, recent survey results suggest that many corporate boards still receive no formal education or training on C&E issues from their firms — a finding that echoes survey findings from the time of the Sarbanes-Oxley Act of 2002 (SOX).[2] With regard to the latter, multiple commentators have certainly pointed out that board service for outside directors is at most a very limited, part-time commitment, typically undertaken by persons with demanding, full-time jobs.[3] And while the people who serve as outside directors often bring substantial business expertise to the role, they are nevertheless highly dependent on management for the information required to perform that role effectively. In context, it should come as no surprise that some critics have decried corporate boards for their limitations in failing to provide a more robust check on management excess — even as others have spoken out as apologists for boards and suggested that the role of directors as part-time outsiders realistically cannot be to "uncover systemic flaws or acts of malfeasance" directly.[4] Regardless of the legal responsibility that directors now have to provide C&E oversight in their firms, these contrasting arguments underline that directors may need more help, education, and empowerment if they are truly expected to perform this oversight function more effectively.

Meanwhile, there appears to be increasing recognition in the business community that the fundamental nature of director oversight is evolving rapidly and that this evolution is essential to restoring public confidence in corporations and their leaders. Recent publications by the Conference Board, the National Association of Corporate Directors, and the Committee for Economic Development all assert that new elements of oversight on the part of directors and boards are required, and that traditional notions of fiduciary responsibility need to evolve to accommodate considerations of risk management, and of C&E, as central parts of directors' role.[5] Whether these new prescriptions represent a basic departure from the traditionalist view of boards (as an exclusive instrument of shareholder interest) or merely a reformulation of what the protection of shareholder interest requires in practice remains to be seen. But either way, these sorts of commentaries have begun to outline new practical considerations for boards as they undertake the task of addressing their emerging new areas of responsibility. Those areas include adopting the necessary infrastructure to drive compliance with law, to build a stronger

---

[2] See Appendix C, John B. Hansen's paper; and Brune, 2003. For Sarbanes-Oxley, see Public Law 107-204, 2002.

[3] See, e.g., Lorsch and Young, 1990.

[4] Cf. Welch and Welch, 2009; and Hurt, 2010.

[5] See Bonime-Blanc and Brevard, 2009; National Association of Corporate Directors, 2009; and Policy and Impact Committee of the Committee for Economic Development, 2010.

ethical culture within organizations, and to ensure that company management undertakes appropriate risk management activity and risk decisionmaking.

Reflections on the evolving nature of board oversight are occurring at a time when the implementation of the C&E function within management is also under close scrutiny. The observation that many C&E programs are check-the-box or merely window-dressing exercises has ramifications that go considerably beyond the role of the board. In fact, in a 2009 symposium that RAND held, "Perspectives of Chief Ethics and Compliance Officers on the Detection and Prevention of Corporate Misdeeds," one of the major take-away points was that the person responsible for running a corporate C&E program (i.e., the chief ethics and compliance officer, or CECO) ideally needs a direct relationship with his/her board in order to better drive effective C&E mechanisms at an operational level.[6] The argument was made that a direct board relationship (by either reporting line or unfiltered access) protects the CECO from undue influence by senior executives and management; makes it possible for him/her to police misbehavior at the highest level of the organization; and supports C&E as a top institutional priority by ensuring that related information is conveyed to the board on a regular basis. This argument suggests that active board involvement in C&E oversight is desirable from an operational viewpoint, regardless of how that involvement fits into the legal notion of fiduciary duty for directors. Put another way, the directors' oversight on C&E may be as important to the success and effectiveness of the CECO and the C&E program as the latter are to the directors' fulfilling their own responsibility and limiting their liability risk.

It is in this context that RAND convened its May 12, 2010, symposium titled "Directors as the Guardians of Ethics and Compliance Within the Corporate Citadel: What the Policy Community Needs to Know." The aim of the symposium was to stimulate a broad conversation about the role of directors in providing C&E oversight in U.S. corporations. The symposium brought together more than two dozen persons, some with distinguished service as directors on leading public company boards, and others with long experience serving as CECOs within firms. Participants also included stakeholders and thought leaders with backgrounds in the non-profit sector, academia, and government. Discussions at the conference focused on challenges and opportunities for boards in performing a C&E oversight role, and on resources and policy that might assist directors in strengthening the C&E function and in more effectively carrying out their oversight responsibility. Participants in the May 2010 RAND symposium are listed in Appendix A of this document, and the conference agenda is reproduced in Appendix B.

Prior to the symposium, three of the invited participants were asked to prepare formal remarks on one of three specific topics: the legal basis of civil liability risk currently faced by corporate directors; the role of the compliance-savvy board from the standpoint of corporate counsel; and the broader need for director oversight of corporate compliance, ethics, culture,

---

[6] See Greenberg, 2009; Boehme, 2009; and Ethics Resource Center, 2007.

and reputational risk. These remarks were then presented in the initial session of the conference. Short summaries of the speakers' remarks are given in Chapter 2, and the white papers on which these remarks were based are reproduced in their entirety in Appendix C.

The second session of the symposium was a moderated discussion on challenges and opportunities for boards in performing the C&E oversight role. Chapter 3 of this document provides a summary of the major themes and topics of conversation in this session.

The final session of the symposium was a moderated discussion on the topic of the empowerment, resources, and policy needed to set up directors to succeed in C&E oversight. Chapter 4 provides a summary of major themes and ideas that were discussed in this session.

2. INVITED REMARKS FROM SYMPOSIUM PARTICIPANTS

The symposium began with remarks from three of the participants in attendance: *Gary Brown*, shareholder, Baker, Donelson, Bearman, Caldwell & Berkowitz, PC; *Jack Hansen*, chair, Compliance and Ethics Committee, Association of Corporate Counsel; and *Keith Darcy*, executive director, Ethics and Compliance Officer Association. Their remarks were based on invited white papers on, respectively, the evolving role and liability of the board of directors for compliance and ethics oversight; the corporate counsel perspective: the crisis of ethics and the need for a compliance-savvy board; and board oversight of compliance, ethics, integrity, and reputation risks: what directors need to know. Each author and topic was selected to bring an important expert viewpoint to, and set the context for, the symposium discussions. Printed in this chapter are short summaries of each set of remarks. The invited white papers are reprinted in their entirety in Appendix C.

Summary of Remarks:
Evolving Role and Liability of the Board of Directors for Ethics and Compliance Oversight

Gary M. Brown, Baker, Donelson, Bearman, Caldwell & Berkowitz, PC

This paper focuses on the responsibility of directors to oversee the ethics and compliance activities of the corporations they serve. This aspect of the director role is relatively new, but is potentially an area in which directors face significant personal exposure. That exposure stems from the combination of the law of fiduciary duty as it applies to directors, together with rapidly evolving standards from the Federal Sentencing Guidelines that define an "effective" compliance and ethics program.

Basic Parameters of Fiduciary Duty for Directors

Under corporate law, one of the basic responsibilities of directors is the duty of care, which obligates them to act with requisite care in managing the corporation's affairs. A key judicial corollary to the duty of care is the business judgment rule, which shelters corporate decisions from judicial second-guessing and litigated hindsight. Where directors have operated in good faith and in pursuit of a rational business purpose, they will typically be protected from liability by the business judgment rule.

Several recent Delaware cases, however, stipulate that the duty of care for directors embraces an affirmative obligation to exercise oversight for corporate compliance activities. Under the *Caremark* (1996) and *Stone v. Ritter* (2006) decisions, a board may not escape liability unless it takes some action to implement a program to detect potential violations of law and corporate policy, and to exercise oversight thereof.

Resonance with the Federal Sentencing Guidelines (FSG)

A key holding in *Caremark* opined that "by establishing and maintaining an effective compliance program, board members can protect themselves from personal liability suits." In the wake of that holding, the 1991 FSG standards for effectiveness in corporate compliance programs quickly became the norm for analyzing potential director liability under *Caremark* as well.

Following the *Stone v. Ritter* affirmation of *Caremark*, it seems likely that the 2004 (and recent 2010) amendments to the FSG will quickly become the standard by which corporate ethics and compliance programs, and the conduct and liability of directors, are judged. The 2004 FSG amendments notably included express responsibility for the board to oversee the corporation's compliance and ethics program; a mandate for the assignment of an individual official to take day-to-day operating responsibility for the compliance and ethics program; and a requirement for a direct reporting channel between that individual and the board.

Learning from the Mistakes of Others

The substance of what is required of boards in overseeing corporate ethics and compliance programs is illustrated through the enforcement activity of various government enforcement agencies, as crystallized in deferred prosecution agreements and consent decrees. Some high-profile examples of firms entering into such agreements in recent years have included Eli Lilly, AstraZeneca, Cephalon, and Bayer.

Common themes that run through related settlement agreements are (1) required direct reporting by the Chief Ethics and Compliance Officer to the board of directors, (2) certification requirements, (3) required periodic assessments of the ethics and compliance programs, and (4) board and management level compliance committees.

Here again, these examples of enforcement standards have the downstream potential to bleed into the calculus of fiduciary duty for boards and, consequently, to contribute to the contours of personal liability for directors.

Observations for Boards

Recent trends in law and enforcement activity merely reinforce what most directors already know — after Enron and Sarbanes-Oxley, it is more important than ever for directors to act diligently in pursuing ethics and compliance oversight. This arguably makes good business sense for the corporation, in that honesty and transparent culture are strong safeguards for shareholder value. These are also safeguards for protecting directors against personal liability. In the face of rapid evolution of relevant law and enforcement standards, the best protection for directors may lie in continuing attention to new precedents, regulatory pronouncements, sentencing standards, etc., in this area.

Summary of Remarks: Corporate Counsel Perspective: The Crisis of Ethics and the Need for a Compliance-Savvy Board

John P. Hansen, Association of Corporate Counsel

In the wake of the financial collapse of 2008, there is substantial evidence that on compliance and ethics issues — the foundation for fostering accountability and trust in business integrity — public companies are not doing a good enough job.

The Problem, as Reflected in an ACC Survey

Late last year, the Compliance and Ethics Committee of the Association of Corporate Counsel (ACC) undertook a survey of 1,600 of its member attorneys. The goal was to take the pulse of the in-house legal community and to learn what corporate counsel are actually doing in the areas of compliance and ethics within their organizations.

- Only half the respondents reported that their organizations assess in any way whether they operate ethically.
- Only half reported providing their boards with compliance or ethics training.
- Seventy-eight percent reported that their organizations never or only rarely undertake ethics risk assessments.

The Moral of the Financial Collapse: When Ethical Shortcuts Become a Business Norm

As Ken Costa, Chairman of Lazard International, has pointed out, many aspects of the financial collapse can be understood as originating from lapses in business integrity. "Liar's loans," conflicts of interest in rating agency operations, and perverse compensation schemes all illustrate failures of accountability and fiduciary responsibility, which became embedded and normalized as ordinary aspects of business practice.

The Elephant in the Room

Although compliance and ethics programs are designed to help mitigate firm risks, ironically, there is one particular risk that such programs can actually create. This is the risk of complacency — the notion that "we've got that base covered." Put another way, it is entirely possible (and all too common) for firms to construct "check-the-box" compliance and ethics programs, which lack a meaningful underlying commitment to accountability, transparency, responsibility, and implementation.

Do boards understand the difference between "checking the box" and a fully robust and effective program? Do they have a working knowledge of what constitutes best ethics and compliance practice in their industry, or the probing questions they should be asking their chief executive officer (CEO) and other senior management? Do they have a plan for how to address legal and ethical concerns that rise through the employee hotline, or other channels, to the top?

A Confluence of Thought Leadership on the Role of Boards

Recent reports published by the National Association of Corporate Directors (NACD), the Conference Board, and the Committee for Economic Development all trumpet related themes with regard to the oversight role for boards on firm ethics, integrity, and risk governance. These (and other) commentators have recommended that boards reassess their related monitoring processes; re-evaluate potentially perverse compensation mechanisms; and make business integrity, culture, and risk issues central in an ongoing dialogue with management.

Creating a Compliance-Savvy Board

In light of the foregoing, board members and management can work toward better compliance and ethics oversight in their companies by acting on several key issues:

- Ensuring appropriate placement of the compliance and ethics function
- Assuring unfiltered access to the board by the individual with day-to-day operational responsibility for ethics and compliance
- Recognizing the influence of organizational culture on business conduct
- Emphasizing the relevance of "ethics" as a subject for risk assessment
- Requiring meaningful board reporting and board education on ethics and compliance matters.

Summary of Remarks:
Board Oversight of Compliance, Ethics, Integrity, and
Reputation Risks: What Directors Need to Know

Keith T. Darcy, Executive Director, Ethics and Compliance Officer Association

As a result of the financial crisis of 2007–2008, the U.S. is undergoing an unprecedented wave of corporate governance and regulatory reforms. Promulgations by regulators, Congress, and the White House are placing new demands on the way corporations are governed. How will these new issues be managed? Are boards prepared and sufficiently informed to step up to heightened expectations, particularly with regard to ethics and compliance oversight for their firms? Will boards necessarily involve their chief ethics and compliance officers (CECOs) as a key resource for meeting the new expectations? And will the increasing and changing requirements for boards, particularly regarding ethics and compliance, ultimately result in reduced risks to the organization?

Federal Sentencing Guidelines and SOX on the Responsibility of Boards for C&E

The fiduciary obligations of the board concerning ethics and compliance programs have been made clear by the Federal Sentencing Guidelines and include, among other things:

- That the board must be knowledgeable about, and exercise reasonable oversight of, the firm's compliance and ethics program
- That there must be a high-level person charged with oversight for the program
- That the individual with operational responsibility for the program must have adequate resources and appropriate authority to execute her/his responsibilities
- That this individual must have direct, unfiltered access to the board
- That the firm must take reasonable steps to communicate appropriate behaviors and conduct effective training for all individuals, including the board.

Directors are also informed of their ethical responsibilities by the Sarbanes-Oxley Act of 2002 (SOX). SOX introduced new standards of accountability for directors of U.S. public companies. Of key importance under SOX is that internal corporate controls are now the direct responsibility of the board, and the failure to establish adequate controls bears significant risks for directors.

The CECO as a Key Resource for Boards on Compliance and Ethics Matters

In the critical area of compliance, integrity, and culture issues, the CECO is the principal agent for the directors in meeting their regulatory and extra-regulatory responsibilities. In order for the CECO to serve as an effective resource for the directors, it is essential that the CECO be an executive-level officer with reporting responsibilities both to the CEO and the board. The CECO must be involved in the day-to-day strategic, operating, and policy decisions of the firm to effectively manage reputation and integrity risks. This kind of responsibility follows from the functions that the CECO is expected to perform, particularly in overseeing the conduct of other top executives and in driving an ethics and compliance agenda at all levels of the firm.

Expanding Board Responsibilities Make the CECO Role Even More Critical

Companies today face a massive new wave of regulation and enforcement, with concomitant risks for firms and their boards. To be effective in overseeing compliance with these new requirements, boards will minimally need (1) knowledge of applicable standards and (2) an empowered CECO. In addition, directors should

- Understand the risks they face as fiduciaries, and how these can be mitigated or resolved
- Recognize and fulfill their responsibilities to oversee the company's management of compliance, ethics, and reputation risks
- Ensure the board agenda includes periodic training on matters of compliance and ethics, including what constitutes an effective program and industry best practice
- Make time on the board agenda, and especially in executive session, for periodic progress reports from the CECO
- Receive briefings on the highest compliance and ethics risks for the company, and what the company is doing to mitigate them
- Make certain the CECO (the person tasked with day-to-day operational management of the program) is an empowered member of senior management with direct, unfiltered access to the board.

Conclusion

With newly heightened expectations for directors to perform ethics and compliance oversight, appointing a strong, independent CECO to act on their behalf is an essential starting point. To do anything less is fraught with peril.

3. CHALLENGES AND OPPORTUNITIES FOR BOARDS IN PERFORMING THE ETHICS AND COMPLIANCE OVERSIGHT ROLE

Participants in this symposium session discussed a broad range of issues connected with the role of corporate directors, the various ways in which ethics and compliance issues relate to the board, and several of the key challenges facing directors in dealing with C&E matters. The session opened with some reflections on the need for directors to balance C&E as an important issue on their radar, but as only one among the many specific demands that are now being placed on directors' time. It was observed that legal, IT, risk, audit, strategy, SOX Section 404 compliance, and obligations under new SEC disclosure rules all represent competing demands for the directors, in addition to their more basic responsibilities concerning review of company performance and protection of shareholder rights. For independent directors who are unlikely to spend more than several weeks a year carrying out their duties, the simple press of time was identified as a significant challenge, both with regard to C&E and for these various other aspects of oversight. Efficiency and effectiveness were therefore stressed as important aims for the directors in husbanding their time and making the strongest possible contribution on C&E.

In a different vein, the opening remarks for the session underlined that directors, in carrying out their responsibilities, help to set the ethical "tone at the top" of their organizations. This basic aspect of what directors do in contributing to organizational culture was identified as being pivotal to their role.

Some of the discussions touched on defining the essence of the ethics and compliance oversight role for directors, on the ways that directors can better inform themselves about C&E matters within the firm, and on the appropriateness and effectiveness of outside legal mandates for board involvement in C&E. The reality that corporate misbehavior and ethically dubious conduct remain abundant in the U.S., despite widespread awareness among directors of these problems, was a major theme of conversation, with a serial focus on several of the potential root causes. Session participants generally agreed on several points:

- The first C&E commandment for directors is "Know Thy Company."
- Ensuring ethical culture is a top responsibility for directors and feeds into other aspects of the director role.
- For directors, the ability to see into C&E matters within the firm is limited and demands putting appropriate management mechanisms into place.
- Although applying ethics to business strategy decisions can sometimes be ambiguous, boards can take concrete steps to improve C&E performance in firms.
- It can be difficult to mandate ethical behavior through the law, but the FSG nevertheless offer critical guidance to boards.

THE FIRST C&E COMMANDMENT FOR DIRECTORS: KNOW THY COMPANY

Independent directors come from a range of different backgrounds, but typically they bring to their board seats a combination of past business experience and technical skills, which are broadly relevant to the oversight of a for-profit organization. What the directors usually do not bring, at least initially, is a deep understanding of the business of their constituent firm. Knowledge of the company and of its industry, of the firm's anatomy and history, and of its operations and unique risks — these are foundational elements of information for the directors, and background that they must acquire in order to function properly in their roles. A working knowledge of the firm and its business model is essential in carrying out all aspects of the directors' role, and a chief and immediate responsibility for each director is to seek out this kind of understanding for the company that he or she serves.

Several participants in the symposium observed that this basic director responsibility to know the company is at least as important for compliance and ethics matters as it is for other aspects of the director role. Some commented that "getting to know" the company provides the backdrop for recognizing what its potential risks and vulnerabilities are. Others observed that "walking around" within the business, speaking directly and candidly with a range of managers and employees, offers a unique avenue for getting a feel for the company and its culture and for where problems might arise. In a complementary vein, another person suggested that directors have a responsibility to keep their "fingers out, but noses in." The observation was made that directors cannot and should not take on direct management responsibility for the operations of the firm, but they need nevertheless to be sufficiently on the ground and connected within the organization to recognize problems and risks, and to be able to raise these as concerns with the senior executives. This kind of effort to know the company was itself identified as a basic ethical commitment on the part of directors, as well as feeding directly into the performance of C&E oversight and risk management for the firm.

Interestingly, a similar point was raised with regard to CECOs, on the management side. It was suggested that in order to function effectively as a CECO, a manager ideally needs to have had some operational experience in the business itself in order to be able to understand the pertinent compliance and ethics issues. More, it was observed that in seeking out information about firm compliance and ethics matters, there is no substitute for a CECO getting out and speaking directly with employees from across the business. At the symposium, one person pointed out that "the stories told around the water cooler" are a very strong indicator of culture and ethical problems within the firm, and that the CECO needs to tap this as a relevant source of information. The alignment between the CECO role and the director role, in this regard, is striking. Knowledge of the company, its culture, and its risks, as perceived by frontline employees and as conveyed through informal conversations during walk-around data collection, is an important resource in C&E oversight. This is true both for directors and for CECOs. By implication, for the directors, the CECO is another key resource for building C&E knowledge about the company, since the CECO has more time, greater access, professional expertise, and inside institutional knowledge in monitoring ethics, compliance, and corporate culture matters.

ENSURING ETHICAL CULTURE IS A TOP RESPONSIBILITY FOR DIRECTORS AND FEEDS INTO OTHER ASPECTS OF THEIR ROLE

Several people at the symposium expressed the view that oversight of culture and ethical values is a fundamental responsibility for directors. This argument follows from the notion that directors help set the "tone at the top," both through their own conduct and supervisory activity and through their responsibility for monitoring senior executives, most notably the CEO. There were mixed opinions about the degree to which directors consistently fulfill this responsibility, however, or even recognize ethics oversight as a basic element of their duty. One participant at the symposium said that independent directors have an obligation to subject all corporate matters that come before them to a "cringe" test: "Whenever a director cringes, that's an indication that there's an ethical problem to be dealt with." Others observed that there are many sources of information that directors ought to be drawing on with regard to assessing the ethical culture of their firms, such as formal and periodic assessments using culture surveys, or the simple expedient of looking at personnel turnover figures from human resources (where given an appropriate industry context, relatively high turnover rates imply potential problems). These sorts of assessments relate more fundamentally to measuring shared values and morale within the firm. Indirectly, they reflect a capacity to detect broader institutional problems in a manner that is qualitatively different from assessing the "cringe-worthiness" of specific business decisions or practices.

In a different vein, it was observed that director oversight of ethical culture is implicitly embedded in many other aspects of what directors do. Hiring of the CEO and review of succession planning; design of appropriate executive compensation mechanisms and incentives; decisions about basic business strategy and risk — all were identified as aspects of the directors' role that have ethical choices and values embedded in them and that contribute to culture within the firm. Where the directors neglect to consider these sorts of oversight activities from an ethical viewpoint, it becomes easy instead to view them in a much narrower and more technical way, thereby running the risk of less ethically desirable outcomes and a more near-sighted management perspective. Over time, the end result could be a corrosive influence on ethical culture within the firm, and a set of conditions under which poor judgment, misbehavior, and scandal are more likely to emerge.

Two other observations were offered in context. First was that a tension sometimes exists around bringing an ethics perspective and a C&E focus to the boardroom. One person said that at least some directors and CEOs "believe that this kind of ethics focus in governance simply gets in the way in conducting business effectively." In this regard, the consensus in the symposium was that while there are some bad and amoral boards, much as there are some bad and amoral chief executives, the general state of the art in directors' practice recognizes that there is a legitimate ethical dimension to the fiduciary duty of directors. Notwithstanding, given the heightened expectations for board oversight of C&E, it was also observed that there is a strong need for better education and awareness of boards concerning both C&E matters and ethical culture. At present, directors are far less likely to seek outside guidance on their C&E responsibilities, for example, than they are on more traditional questions concerning governance and strategy. It was suggested that many directors could benefit from new training opportunities to clarify how their own personal commitments to integrity and board service can translate into a more conscious focus on C&E in the boardroom and on ethical culture in the firm.[1]

FOR DIRECTORS, THE ABILITY TO SEE INTO C&E MATTERS WITHIN THE FIRM IS LIMITED AND DEMANDS PUTTING APPROPRIATE MECHANISMS IN PLACE

One theme repeatedly observed in the symposium was that in some basic sense, directors have very limited resources for obtaining information within the firm, and they depend for information partly on the same executives whom they oversee. With regard to compliance risk, for example, one person offered the example that "it's impossible to expect directors to ask the right questions of senior management, where the latter are involved in a calculated effort to manipulate the books and to conceal having done so from the outside world." Another person observed that if the task of the board is to manage ethics and compliance lapses, then surely the first step in doing so is to put appropriate controls and mechanisms in place within management. It was suggested that even ordinarily upstanding corporate employees sometimes "behave badly when the lights are off," and that this reflects an inherent weakness in human nature. Consequently, the board's responsibility is "to make sure that the lights always stay on," that transparency within the corporation is fully maintained, and that "the internal signal for doing the right thing" is strongly broadcast throughout the organization.

These comments link back, in turn, to the remarks that Keith Darcy and others offered on CECOs. They observed that the board should not be operating in a vacuum when it reviews ethics and compliance matters. Rather, the standards for C&E oversight laid out in the Federal Sentencing Guidelines contemplate that there will be a designated official with responsibility to lead C&E from within management (i.e., the CECO) and, in turn, that the board would have direct, unfiltered access to that person in order to carry out its oversight responsibilities. It was suggested that in much the same way that the general counsel advises the board on legal matters, or the chief financial officer (CFO) on financial matters, the CECO advises the board on compliance and ethics matters. That means that the CECO becomes primarily responsible for designing and implementing the mechanisms to ensure compliance with law and to foster ethical culture within the firm — and serves partly as the agent for the board in carrying this out. More, regular contacts between the board and the CECO serve to create a reporting channel so that directors do receive relevant performance information on C&E, as well as a focus for

[1] In regard to the standards for board training issues, see Boehme, 2010.

ongoing dialogue among the directors about what the most pressing compliance and ethics risks within the company are, and how these relate to business operations and strategy.

ALTHOUGH APPLYING ETHICS TO BUSINESS STRATEGY DECISIONS CAN SOMETIMES BE AMBIGUOUS, BOARDS CAN NEVERTHELESS TAKE CONCRETE STEPS TO IMPROVE C&E PERFORMANCE IN FIRMS

Another theme that emerged in conversation was the contrast between the ambiguity of how ethics should apply to board oversight of business strategy and the clarity of steps that can be taken by boards to improve C&E practice within their firms. Regarding the former, there were differences of opinion in the symposium about whether ethics are easy or difficult for directors in the boardroom to apply. One person suggested that "most directors tend to think of themselves as ethically upstanding, but that different people have very different ideas about what ethics calls for in practice." Several people observed that beyond a basic commitment to personal integrity and honesty, it is not at all clear how directors are supposed to apply ethical principles to big-picture questions involving business dealings, or even who gets to decide what the relevant ethical principles ought to be. One person asserted that directors ought periodically "to challenge management to comment on ethical considerations in the business, and that that conversation ought to embrace ... day-to-day operating concerns, as well as big picture strategy questions." Another person expressed a somewhat contrasting view, which is that for directors, risk management may be a more tractable topic to address than "ethics" and, by extension, represents a higher priority for the board.

A third person offered a very different and competing observation about the directors' role. He suggested that directors need to think about C&E "not just as an abstract consideration in the boardroom, but in light of the reality that corporate crime and corruption are widespread." Regardless of any ambiguity around the application of ethics in boardroom deliberations about strategy, directors have a clear responsibility to recognize the problems of crime and corruption and the potential for these to manifest within their own organizations. It was further suggested that directors operating on their own are very unlikely to unearth significant instances of corruption or collusion until too late. Again, it was suggested that the directors' role is to ensure that appropriate controls and mechanisms are put in place within the firm, in advance, to prevent misconduct or to detect it as early as possible. More, director oversight on C&E helps to ensure that these mechanisms continue to function as they should, and that any major compliance problems that are detected get brought to the directors' attention for redress.

This perspective on directors and C&E, and on the prevention of criminal misconduct, implies a set of tangible steps that directors can take to fulfill their duties. Here again, ensuring the appointment of an effective senior-level CECO, someone with day-to-day responsibility for the C&E function and the resources needed to carry it out, is an important initial step for the board. Among other things, the CECO serves to drive related data-gathering, investigation, and enforcement activities from within management and feeds information from those activities back to the directors. In turn, obtaining and reviewing data from these sorts of compliance activities, and assessing the company's performance, are another concrete step that fits well within the directors' role. Seeking out appropriate training on C&E matters, responsive to the evolving nature of board oversight responsibility, is still another step that directors can take, potentially with advice and support from the CECO. Finally, directors might consider other sorts of steps to strengthen C&E mechanisms in firms, such as building C&E performance criteria into compensation mechanisms for managers and creating incentives for superior achievement based on quantifiable performance targets.

IT CAN BE DIFFICULT TO MANDATE ETHICAL BEHAVIOR THROUGH THE LAW, BUT THE FEDERAL SENTENCING GUIDELINES OFFER CRITICAL GUIDANCE TO BOARDS

One significant observation shared at the symposium was that it is very difficult to mandate ethics and that subjecting directors to new legal requirements and obligations on C&E is likely to be counterproductive. One person observed that "ethics laws only bind the ethical" and that mandates to directors (and executives) can easily fall flat for that reason. Another suggested that overburdening directors with responsibility or liability on C&E matters could make it more difficult to find qualified people willing to serve in this role — a counter-productive result. A third person suggested that new legal and regulatory mandates for directors could easily lead in the direction of boards attempting narrowly to meet requirements on paper, while losing the underlying spirit in which the requirements were promulgated — again, a paradoxical result for ethics and compliance purposes. A fourth person said that more government regulation is unlikely to assist companies and boards in carrying out C&E responsibility and that the more telling issue is how to empower boards, rather than compel them, on these issues.

In light of these comments, several of the compliance and ethics experts in the symposium room suggested that the strength of the current Federal Sentencing Guidelines on C&E primarily flows from laying out specific parameters for what a good C&E program should look like and how the board should be connected to that program. In one important sense, the FSG standards serve as a how-to guide for the directors to ensure that reasonable C&E mechanisms are effectively established within their firms. Arguably, that kind of guidance from the FSG might be as important as the threat of criminal sanction to the company or of civil liability for directors under state corporate law. Put another way, a key element of policy embedded in the FSG involves a simple articulation for directors and executives about how to carry out the C&E responsibility. And although some government rules on C&E potentially can create the risk of paradoxical results, such as a narrowly technical focus among executives in meeting legal requirements on paper, in this instance, the FSG may actually be helpful to directors who are searching for a blueprint of what an effective C&E program should look like.

4. EMPOWERMENT, RESOURCES, AND POLICY: HOW DO WE SET DIRECTORS UP TO SUCCEED IN ETHICS AND COMPLIANCE OVERSIGHT?

Participants in the final session of the symposium focused more deeply on the topics of board empowerment and policy and on ways to facilitate and encourage directors in playing a stronger C&E oversight role. One focus of the discussion touched on government enforcement authority and liability risk pertaining to C&E matters and the incentives these policies create for persons serving as directors. The reality was underscored that boards face heightened civil liability on compliance and ethics, resulting from a combination of recent legal and regulatory developments. It was also observed that there is serious interest in the regulatory community in facilitating board engagement on compliance and ethics oversight, as well as concern that some boards and directors really are not digging into these issues deeply enough. The question was raised, How can the policy community help in promoting stronger recognition of C&E issues in the director community, and better related performance by boards and by management? Some pragmatic steps along these lines, such as director certifications in C&E or bringing people with C&E backgrounds onto boards as outside directors, were discussed. Another theme of discussion involved some of the specific steps that managers and CECOs can take in building stronger C&E programs within firms. It was noted that although these kinds of programmatic steps are somewhat removed from the immediate role of the directors, familiarity with the elements of a strong C&E program can help boards in asking the right questions of CECOs and in confirming that the right sorts of controls and institutional mechanisms are put in place.

Several of the major points of discussion and agreement during the session included the following:

- The Federal Sentencing Guidelines have created more oversight responsibility and liability risk for directors, so more robust, targeted board education on C&E is needed.
- Fiduciary duty calls for a robust decisionmaking process on C&E.
- Empowering the CECO is a path to empowering the board.
- Boards should seek out multiple sources of information and reporting on C&E.
- More specific feedback from regulators, citing cases in which companies benefited from specific, strong C&E program steps, would drive more-effective corporate programs.
- The "conversation" between directors and the CECO is a key asset for the board.

THE FEDERAL SENTENCING GUIDELINES HAVE CREATED MORE OVERSIGHT RESPONSIBILITY AND LIABILITY RISK FOR DIRECTORS, SO MORE ROBUST, TARGETED BOARD EDUCATION ON C&E IS NEEDED

One basic observation made in the symposium was that the Sarbanes-Oxley Act of 2002 "did not, by itself, put directors at increased risk in regard to compliance and ethics activity." Although many of the SOX prescriptions had major effects on corporate executives and operations, such as the requirements for whistleblower protection mechanisms (§806), stronger internal controls and reporting processes (§404), and officer certifications (§302), those provisions did not impinge directly on boards, their scope of oversight, or their risk. What eventually did impact boards were the provisions under SOX that called for review of the Federal Sentencing Guidelines rules on organizational crime. Corresponding revisions were made in 2004, which emphasized the importance of achieving an ethical corporate culture, expanded considerably on the definitions for what a corporate C&E program needs to look like, and highlighted the responsibility of the board of directors in connection with such a program.[1] The immediate effect of the FSG amendments was to create incentives for corporations to implement strong C&E programs in compliance with the guidelines in order to qualify for leniency in sentencing in the event of subsequent misconduct. The indirect effect, in theory, should have been to prevent instances of misconduct in the private sector by cultivating stronger compliance mechanisms and better ethical culture in the first instance.

For directors, another effect was heightened risk for civil liability under state law. The major Delaware precedents of *Caremark* and *Stone v. Ritter* set the stage for director liability for C&E by establishing that the fiduciary duty of directors includes a responsibility to ensure that C&E matters really are being addressed programmatically within the firm. In practice, the details for what is actually required of firms and, by extension, of directors have been filled in by the Federal Sentencing Guidelines. It was observed in the symposium that the most recent amendments to the FSG are likely to augment the yardstick by which states gauge the duty of directors on C&E oversight by emphasizing direct and unfiltered access between the CECO and the board and by underscoring the need for the board to take an active, independent oversight role on C&E. By implication, where directors neglect to live up to the monitoring standards laid out in the FSG, they are at risk of violating state law fiduciary requirements as well, and may be subject to civil suits accordingly.

One strand of discussion in the symposium implicitly questioned whether this kind of liability for directors is a good idea, whether it's likely to move directors and firms in a positive direction, and whether it might have the unintended effect of discouraging qualified candidates from serving on public company boards. A more robust strand of discussion focused on the

---

[1] As pointed out by two of the papers (Brown's and Darcy's; see Appendix C) for the symposium, the 2004 amendments to the FSG specifically address the responsibility of directors in "requiring that board be knowledgeable about the content and operation of the C&E program" and that directors "must reasonably oversee the implementation and effectiveness of the program."

reality that the current legal framework does place boards at risk and, consequently, that directors need to be cognizant of this fact as they carry out their responsibilities. It was suggested by several in the symposium that in fact many directors don't recognize the risk they face on C&E and don't understand the legal framework from which it originates. Here again, recent survey results were noted suggesting that only a minority of companies undertake any formal education or training for their boards on C&E matters.[2] Better education and training for directors on these issues, and particularly on the threshold concern of civil liability, were identified as a high priority for firms and boards in the future.

FIDUCIARY DUTY CALLS FOR A ROBUST DECISIONMAKING PROCESS ON C&E

Another theme raised in this session involved the nature of directors' fiduciary duty with regard to overseeing C&E within the firm. For purposes of liability risk, it was observed that directors are not themselves required to make primary decisions about ethics and compliance in the firm. Rather, the directors' obligation under *Caremark* and *Stone* is mainly to ensure that processes are put in place in order to build effective C&E into management. So for purposes of civil liability risk, the immediate challenge for directors is not any of the abstruse questions about how ethics should enter into discussions of business strategy, or how ethics relate to the fundamental role of being a director, or how to implement good C&E practice on a daily basis in the firm. As always, the directors are separate from management and removed from day-to-day operational decisions. Instead, what fiduciary duty calls for is a recognition that C&E is a part of the monitoring responsibility of the board and that the directors need to make sure that an agent within management is appropriately tasked and resourced to carry this function out. In the symposium session, a distinction was drawn between directors "doing nothing" on C&E and "deciding to do nothing." The latter connotes that the directors are carrying out their C&E monitoring responsibility and that the necessary C&E mechanisms have been put in place, even though the board does not itself make operational or implementation decisions.

Once again, a major implication from the symposium is that directors are not expected to operate in a vacuum on C&E and that much of the mechanics and operational side of running a good C&E program will occur at the management level, rather than at the board level. Effective reporting mechanisms (including a robust system for investigations and follow-up), effective anti-retaliation policies, strong C&E training and communication across the organization, organizational risk and culture assessments and regular data gathering, consistent and transparent disciplinary processes, appropriate investigations when needed, etc. — all of these are elements of what goes into a strong C&E program. The board is not directly responsible for the details of these elements, nor do the directors need to understand all the nuances of implementation surrounding them. What the board does need to do is to make sure that a senior-level, competent, and well-resourced person is leading the development and oversight of

---

[2] See Hansen's paper in Appendix C.

these various mechanisms. Ideally, that person should have a direct, unfiltered relationship with the board[3] in order to report back on the adequacy of all the procedural steps on C&E, as well as on any specific gaps or challenges that arise within the company over time.

Two people in the symposium session commented that boards should be "holding [their] CEOs accountable on C&E performance issues within the firm." Several others observed that beyond holding the CEO to account on this, the board ought to have a direct relationship with the person who exercises day-to-day responsibility for the C&E program — again, the CECO. Beyond the fact that this can contribute to liability protection for the board, it means that the board has an in-house expert to consult with on a full range of ethics and compliance questions — including what sorts of education or training might be appropriate for the board itself. Again, the take-away point is that the board does not need to operate by itself, or to know all the answers on C&E, or to understand how to implement a C&E program and controls within management. Rather, the CECO is supposed to be the go-to person for the board on these matters, and the board carries out a major part of its responsibility simply by making sure that role is filled appropriately and resourced correctly, and then engaging in a regular dialogue with that person.

EMPOWERING THE CECO IS A PATH TO EMPOWERING THE BOARD

The newest proposed amendments to the Federal Sentencing Guidelines reinforce the notion that a direct relationship between the board and the CECO is a key element needed to empower robust board oversight on C&E.[4] The guidelines stipulate that the existence of this relationship will be considered as a mitigating factor in criminal sentencing for organizations. One question that this invites is, Why? In the symposium, it was observed that the structure of the CECO position, and who that person reports to, is central in determining how effective the CECO will be and, ultimately, in defining the parameters of the C&E program. When the CECO reports to the board, one implication is that the board receives a flow of information, unfiltered, that it otherwise would not. Another implication is that the CECO becomes more independent, and more protected from executive influence than he or she otherwise would be. The latter is important given that one of the CECO's potential functions is to detect misconduct at the highest levels of the organization and to pass corresponding information back to the board for action if needed. Likewise, when the CECO reports to the board (and to the top executives) on C&E matters, that has the likely effect of elevating the C&E role within the hierarchy of the organization. The CECO becomes more likely to contribute an ethics or "long-view" perspective

---

[3] In this regard, the proposed 2010 revisions to the FSG would create direct incentives for an unfiltered reporting channel between the board and the CECO. See U.S. Sentencing Commission, 2010, p. 18.

[4] The newest revisions to the FSG are slated to become effective on November 1, 2010. For details, background, and commentary, see U.S. Sentencing Commission, 2010, p. 18.

to strategic decisionmaking in the C-suite, and to building ethical culture across the organization, to the extent that he or she has the backing of the board in this way.

In the symposium, it was also noted that a major related challenge that firms and boards face in risk management is "siloing," or the division of responsibility across multiple internal fiefdoms that do not integrate well. In a related vein, when ethics and compliance concerns are buried in an internal management silo, and particularly when these functions are several levels down the management hierarchy from senior leadership, the likelihood that the CECO can drive a strong C&E program that cuts across corporate silos is reduced. In principle, when the CECO has a direct relationship with the board, is a senior executive in his/her own right, and is positioned in a way not subordinate to other management functions (like HR, audit, or legal), the CECO is better positioned to press a C&E agenda across the organization. Many of the mandates in the Federal Sentencing Guidelines concerning the structure of C&E programs implicitly draw on these sorts of considerations, which is another reason why a direct relationship between the board and the CECO is emphasized.

Consonant with the foregoing, a major theme raised in the symposium was the notion that the board and the CECO potentially have a mutually enabling relationship. The board empowers the CECO by creating a reporting channel, by conveying the message that C&E is a top priority for the organization to address, and by ensuring that the person who fills the CECO role has the mandate and resources to carry it out effectively. In turn, the CECO empowers the board by acting as its agent on these concerns, by creating a robust flow of information and performance data back to the board, and by bringing ethics and compliance issues before the board as a regular topic of conversation. Arguably then, the CECO and board are interdependent: the success of each, on C&E matters, may depend upon the other. In a somewhat related vein, several people in the symposium observed that a successful board needs to cultivate relationships with multiple senior executives, rather than "relying on the CEO as its intermediary and sole source for securing information about the company." Ideally, the board needs to be able to reach out directly to the heads of HR, finance, legal, risk management, and other divisions in order to have more and better information from multiple sources within the organization. Ideally, the CECO should be one of those key resources for the board, and the one who empowers the board to ask questions about C&E of all the other division heads.

MORE SPECIFIC FEEDBACK FROM REGULATORS, CITING CASES IN WHICH COMPANIES BENEFITED FROM SPECIFIC, STRONG C&E PROGRAM STEPS, WOULD DRIVE MORE-EFFECTIVE CORPORATE PROGRAMS

Discussion in this session began with a focus on the regulatory perspective on boards, compliance, and ethics. It was observed that regulators today are concerned with many issues of illegal conduct and poor risk management on the part of corporations, and are very interested in boards and directors as a private-sector front line in seeking to address these problems. Recent developments in fiduciary case law for directors, taken together with evolving standards on C&E from multiple sources, have the impact of pressing directors toward a more proactive stance on C&E, and management toward an explicit C&E agenda. Ambivalence was expressed in the symposium about whether these sorts of legal requirements and mandates for directors are a good thing from the standpoint of those serving on boards. Some felt that directors may be subject to too much liability risk and to too many demands, given the limitations of their part-time oversight role. It was also suggested that "ethics laws only bind the ethical," that imposing too many C&E rules on directors could lead to an unduly technical and self-interested perspective on risk, and that increasing liability for directors has the potential to undermine the labor market for people willing to serve. In light of these considerations, there was skepticism in the room about whether more regulation concerning boards and C&E would be useful, and some sentiment that it could easily become self-defeating.

One contrasting suggestion that was made was that stronger regulatory involvement in citing positive examples of C&E accomplishment could be very helpful.[5] It was suggested that particularly where specific C&E mechanisms, program features, or board involvement are seen by agencies as having prevented major problems or as having mitigated instances of criminal misconduct, communicating this information back to the corporate community could have a significant positive impact on behavior. This kind of communication could help broadly to elevate consciousness about C&E issues among directors and senior managers while providing good examples and case studies for them to follow in dealing with different sorts of problems. One symposium participant noted that it would be helpful for the private sector to have access to formal statistics from the SEC, DOJ, and other agencies about all of the instances in which good C&E practices led to deferred prosecution, lesser sentencing, reduced penalties, etc., as those kinds of data could help to make a more quantitative case for the value return of good C&E for the corporate bottom line. Another person commented that there had been one or two specific instances in the past few years where the SEC actually had publicized positive accomplishments in C&E programs in the context of specific investigations of specific companies. It was suggested, though, that much more could be done by regulators along these lines.

This thread of conversation highlighted the sense that regulators ought, in some sense, to be involved in an ongoing dialogue with the business community around C&E issues. Apart from the direct impact of regulators in writing new rules, conducting enforcement actions, or imposing punitive sanctions, a dialogue between regulators and the business community could help shape consensus around what works in C&E (and what does not), what the role of directors and managers is and ought to be, and what kinds of emerging C&E problems the business community will be facing in the future. Policymakers have the opportunity to influence business by providing it with data and candid information and by listening, as well.

---

[5] On this point, see also Murphy, 2009.

Ultimately, that kind of dialogue could have a positive impact on boards and firms regardless of views on the merits of increased liability risk for directors or new forms of regulatory intervention.

THE CONVERSATION BETWEEN DIRECTORS AND THE CECO IS A KEY ASSET FOR THE BOARD

The concluding theme of discussion in the symposium touched on the value of the CECO as a conversation starter for the board and as a point of departure for directors in asking questions and seeking answers on a broad range of ethics and compliance issues. It was observed in the symposium that even as the responsibility of directors on ethics and compliance matters has escalated, directors' understanding remains limited for what that responsibility means in practice. The CECO should serve as a primary resource for empowering the directors, both in dealing with these sorts of issues and, more fundamentally, in posing related questions and getting answers. To the extent that there is an information gap for directors at the outset, a lack of basic familiarity for what the C&E oversight role is and for how to carry it out, the CECO should be the go-to resource to help fill that gap. So, for example, when directors have concerns about, or a need for, board education on C&E matters, the CECO is a key resource for delivering basic information on effective compliance programs, current resources and trends, best practices by peers and industry, benchmarking performance, etc. More, the CECO is also the resource for identifying appropriate additional training materials and opportunities, and even for challenging directors to seek out this kind of education and support. One person observed, and others agreed, that the CECO "can help the directors by prompting them with the questions that they should be asking of management on compliance and ethics matters." In this regard, several of the symposium participants offered to share an illustrative, canonical list of C&E questions for directors, which is included in this document as Appendix D.

Obviously, in posing questions to the CECO and to other managers, the board immediately begins to fulfill its own oversight responsibility. More, the opportunity to engage the CECO in this kind of discussion offers an avenue for the directors to address other ethics concerns that uniquely arise in the boardroom setting. To the extent that directors find themselves grappling with basic ethical questions as a matter of business strategy, or have concerns about how to raise C&E issues effectively with their peers, or want to understand the process for building an "ethical culture" within the company, the CECO is a point person who can (and should) be asked about any of these matters. When a C&E crisis hits, the CECO should work closely with the board (and with other executives) to address it appropriately and to take remedial action. The ability of the directors to rely on the CECO in this way depends on their forming a relationship and reaching a comfort level with that person in advance. Thus, establishing a conversation with the CECO can potentially be useful to the directors in many different ways over time.

APPENDIX A: SYMPOSIUM PARTICIPANTS

Michael Greenberg (Symposium Chair)
Director, RAND Center for Corporate Ethics and Governance

Donna C. Boehme (Symposium Co-Chair)
Principal, Compliance Strategists, LLC

Urmi Ashar
President and Chief Executive Officer, National Association of Corporate Directors, Three Rivers Chapter

J. Troy Beatty
Branch Chief for Comparative Law and Regulation and Lead FCPA Counsel, Office of International Affairs, U.S. Securities and Exchange Commission

Gary M. Brown
Shareholder, Baker, Donelson, Bearman, Caldwell & Berkowitz, PC

Lovida H. Coleman Jr.
Director, RiskMetrics Group

Keith T. Darcy
Executive Director, Ethics and Compliance Officer Association

Roxanne Decyk
Executive Vice President, Global Government Relations, Shell Oil Company

James N. Dertouzos
Director, RAND Institute for Civil Justice

Blane Erwin
Vice President, Strategic Initiatives, Bridgeway

Bruce F. Freed
President, Center for Political Accountability

Peter Gleason
Managing Director and Chief Financial Officer, National Association of Corporate Directors

Patrick J. Gnazzo
Senior Vice President and General Manager, U.S. Public Sector, CA, Inc.

John P. (Jack) Hansen
Executive Fellow, Center for Business Ethics, Bentley University; Chair, Compliance and Ethics Committee of the Association of Corporate Counsel

Ann McLaughlin Korologos
Trustee, RAND Corporation; former U.S. Secretary of Labor

Matthew Lepore
Vice President, Chief Counsel — Corporate Governance, and Assistant General Counsel, Pfizer Inc.

Michael Meltzer
Chief Executive Officer, Sirota Survey Intelligence®

Cindy Moehring
Vice President and Chief Ethics Officer, Wal-Mart Stores, Inc.

George Muñoz
Partner, Tobin, Petkus & Muñoz; co-founder, Muñoz Investment Banking Group

Joseph Murphy
Director of Public Policy, Society of Corporate Compliance and Ethics

Shirley Peterson
Director, The Goodyear Tire & Rubber Co., AK Steel Corp., and Wolverine World Wide, Inc.

Christopher D. Petitt
Founder, Blue Haystack, Inc.

Robert F. Roach
Chief Compliance Officer, New York University

Harold J. Tinkler
Former Chief Ethics and Compliance Officer, Deloitte LLP and the Deloitte U.S. Firms

Alan Yuspeh
Senior Vice President and Chief Ethics and Compliance Officer, Hospital Corporation of America Inc.

Larry Zicklin
Clinical Professor of Business Ethics, Leonard N. Stern School of Business, New York University

APPENDIX B: SYMPOSIUM AGENDA

Directors as Guardians of Compliance and Ethics Within the Corporate Citadel: What the Policy Community Should Know

Ritz Carlton, Pentagon City

1250 South Hayes Street, Arlington, VA 22202; Tel: (703) 415-5000

May 12, 2010

Symposium Chair: Dr. Michael Greenberg *Symposium Co-Chair: Donna C. Boehme*

1:00 p.m. **Welcome and Introductory Remarks**

Lawrence Zicklin, Clinical Professor of Business Ethics, Leonard N. Stern School of Business, New York University; former Chairman of the Board, Neuberger Berman

Michael Greenberg, Director, RAND Center for Corporate Ethics and Governance

1:10 p.m. **Invited Remarks from Three Panelists**

Introductions by Donna C. Boehme, Principal of Compliance Strategists, LLC

- Evolving Role and Liability of the Board of Directors for Ethics and Compliance Oversight — Gary Brown, Shareholder, Baker, Donelson, Bearman, Caldwell & Berkowitz, PC
- Corporate Counsel Perspective: The Crisis of Ethics and the Need for a Compliance-Savvy Board — Jack Hansen, Chair, Compliance and Ethics Committee, Association of Corporate Counsel
- Board Oversight of Compliance, Ethics, Integrity, and Reputation Risks: What Directors Need to Know — Keith Darcy, Executive Director, Ethics and Compliance Officer Association

2:00 p.m. **Discussion Session 1: Challenges and Opportunities for Boards in Performing the Ethics and Compliance Oversight Role**

Introductory Remarks: Peter Gleason, Managing Director and Chief Financial Officer, National Association of Corporate Directors

3:15 p.m. **Break**

3:25 p.m. **Discussion Session 2: Empowerment, Resources and Policy: How Do We Set Directors Up to Succeed in Ethics and Compliance Oversight?**

Introductory Remarks: J. Troy Beatty, Branch Chief for Comparative Law and Regulation and Lead FCPA Counsel, Office of International Affairs, U.S. Securities and Exchange Commission

4:40 p.m. **Closing Remarks**

Michael Greenberg, RAND Corporation

5:00 p.m. **Reception** *(concluding at 6:00 p.m.)*

APPENDIX C: INVITED PAPERS FROM PANEL PARTICIPANTS

EVOLVING ROLE AND LIABILITY OF THE BOARD OF DIRECTORS FOR ETHICS AND COMPLIANCE OVERSIGHT

Gary M. Brown, *Baker, Donelson, Bearman, Caldwell & Berkowitz, PC*
Remarks presented on May 12, 2010

In the post-Enron, post financial crisis world of 2010, the oversight responsibilities of corporate directors are evolving rapidly. Although the traditional state-law fiduciary requirements for directors, i.e., good faith, duty of care, and duty of loyalty, remain very much in place, the meaning and application of those requirements, particularly in the ethics and compliance arena are posing new challenges and opportunities for corporate directors.

This paper focuses on the responsibility of directors to oversee the ethics and compliance activities of the corporations they serve. This aspect of the director role is relatively new and little discussed; however, it is potentially one of the principal areas in which corporate directors face significant personal exposure. To grasp the potential for liability, as well as the expectations for corporate boards, requires an appreciation for the law of fiduciary duty as it relates to directors, and how that law interfaces with the U.S. Federal Sentencing Guidelines (FSG) parameters for an effective ethics and compliance program.

Rapid evolution of applicable legal standards complicates directors' obligations in this regard. The 2004 amendments and proposed 2010 amendments to the FSG juxtapose atop significant judicial developments relative to director oversight duties. More, directors must remain constantly attentive to the compliance programs that they oversee as new agency pronouncements and high-profile settlement agreements provide new insights on "effective" compliance practice and, by extension, on the directors' oversight role.

In sum, directors' responsibility for ethics and compliance oversight emerges from a confluence of many different sources of law and enforcement authority, including major Delaware judicial precedents, statutory directives of the Sarbanes-Oxley Act that resulted in changes to the FSG, and prominent deferred prosecution agreements (DPAs) and corporate integrity agreements (CIAs) involving companies such as Eli Lilly, Bayer and AstraZeneca.[1]

Collectively, these various pronouncements suggest that directors have considerable responsibility when it comes to oversight of ethics and compliance matters, and that directors and their firms can be held accountable for deficiencies in that oversight. These responsibilities

---

[1] Note that in addition to the foregoing, prosecutorial policies as expressed in Department of Justice memoranda (i.e., the "Thompson/Holder/McNulty memos") set forth complementary standards for when corporations will be prosecuted for organizational crime. Effective ethics and compliance policies in the corporation are a central factor in DOJ's decision-making here.

exist alongside, and in the context of, more general parameters for the director role, such as the duty of care and the business judgment rule. I begin an analysis of director responsibility for ethics and compliance oversight by quickly touching on some foundational concepts.

Basic Parameters of Fiduciary Duty for Corporate Directors

Under corporate law, the basic responsibility of directors is the *duty of care*, with its judicial corollary, the *business judgment rule*. In essence, the notion of *duty of care* suggests that the responsibility of directors goes beyond mere loyalty and the avoidance of self-dealing, and includes an obligation to act with the requisite degree of care in managing the corporation's affairs. Whether the duty of care is met in a particular situation requires complex fact-intensive analysis of many factors (e.g., complexity of the enterprise, time devoted by the director, homework and inquiry, etc.). The standard usually applied by courts to determine whether a director has violated the duty of care is gross negligence.[2]

In practice, a failure to use due care does not alone establish liability for directors. Instead, it has the effect of rebutting the presumption of the business judgment rule as a defense. Broadly speaking, the business judgment rule reflects a fundamental judicial acknowledgment that the directors of a corporation are responsible for managing a business, where undertaking risk to obtain profit is a fundamental purpose of the corporation's existence. The rule thus shelters ordinary corporate decisions from judicial second-guessing and litigated hindsight.[3] Under the business judgment rule, directors' decisions will typically be respected by courts unless the directors lack independence, act in bad faith or in a manner that cannot be attributed to a rational business purpose, or else reach a business decision by a grossly negligent process that fails to consider material facts reasonably available.[4]

Finally, there is one other matter that corporate directors cannot overlook — that is the requirement to act in "good faith." The notion of "good faith" always has been a part of the fiduciary obligations of corporate directors and is codified as a required element of the conduct of directors. "Good faith" has arisen in the context of whether directors are entitled to business judgment rule protection, a basic requirement of which is that one *exercise* business judgment. There is a critical distinction between *doing nothing* (which is not "acting in good faith") and *deciding to do nothing*. The latter gets business judgment rule protection; the former does not.

Analysis of the application of the business judgment rule and the related legal concept of good faith can rapidly become a very technical exercise. But the basic premise under the case law is that directors have a lot of protection against civil liability for their decisions and actions that comply with the business judgment rule and with the duty of care. Other complementary

---

[2] See *Smith v. Van Gorkom*, 488 A.2d 858 (Del. 1985).

[3] For one widely cited articulation of the business judgment rule under Delaware law, see *Aronson v. Lewis*, 473 A.2d 805 (Del. 1984).

[4] See, e.g., *Emerald Partners v. Berlin*, 787 A.2d 85 (Del. 2001); *Unocal Corp. v. Mesa Petroleum Co.*, 483 A.2d 946 (Del. 1985).

sources of protection for directors, such as exculpatory provisions under corporate charters, only serve to enhance that basic protection from civil liability.

So, in light of this general context, from whence does director responsibility for ethics and compliance oversight spring? And what risks do directors face in connection with that responsibility?

The Duty to Monitor — *Caremark; Stone v. Ritter;* Citigroup

In 1996, the Delaware Court of Chancery's *Caremark* decision suggested that directors have an affirmative obligation to exercise oversight of corporate compliance activities.[5] In *Caremark,* Chancellor Allen indicated that substantial failure to exercise that oversight undercuts the claim of good faith necessary for directors to invoke the business judgment rule.

Since the *Caremark* decision, directors' fiduciary duties have been understood to embrace the adoption and maintenance of corporate compliance programs designed to detect corporate wrongdoing and bring it to the attention of management and the board of directors. In 2006, the Delaware Supreme Court revisited and clarified the issue in *Stone v. Ritter,*[6] which adopted and clarified *Caremark*'s standard for determining directors' oversight liability. *Stone* involved a derivative action by shareholders of AmSouth Bancorporation, following the disclosure of violations by AmSouth of the federal Bank Secrecy Act. The lawsuit alleged that the directors of AmSouth had breached their duty to act in good faith because, while AmSouth maintained a program to monitor Bank Secrecy Act compliance, the program had not been adequate to prevent the violations.

In dismissing the case against the directors, the Delaware Supreme Court ruled that the *Caremark* standard is the appropriate standard for director duties with respect to corporate compliance issues. The *Caremark* standard establishes that a Board may not escape liability unless it took some actions to implement a program to detect potential violations of law and corporate policy and to exercise a duty of oversight. More, this is understood to require that the compliance program incorporate procedures by which the Board can track and analyze compliance problems that arise and take steps to ensure that they do not continue or recur. The *Stone* Court further confirmed *Caremark*'s statement that board liability could be imposed only for "a sustained or systematic failure of the board to exercise oversight — such as an utter failure to attempt to assure a reasonable information and reporting system exists" or for a decision to ignore "red flags," and conditioned any finding of such liability on the directors' knowledge that they were violating their fiduciary duties. The *Caremark/Stone* analysis was recently re-affirmed in dismissing claims against Citigroup directors, who were alleged to have

---

[5] See *In re Caremark International Inc. Derivative Litigation,* 698 A.2d 959 (Del. Ch. 1996).
[6] *Stone v. Ritter,* 911 A.2d 362 (2006).

breached their oversight duties, leading to the massive losses during the recent financial markets meltdown.[7]

The Federal Sentencing Guidelines — Ethics and Compliance Programs

The sentiments expressed in *Caremark* and its progeny have a great resonance in the legislative and regulatory environment that has existed since 2002. The Sarbanes-Oxley Act of 2002, the SEC's rules and regulations adopted thereunder, and the listing standard of the national stock exchanges require, among other things "disclosure controls and procedures," and corporations now are required to certify, and have their auditors attest to the adequacy of, the corporation's internal control over financial reporting.

For purposes of director liability, perhaps the most important provisions of Sarbanes-Oxley are sections 805 and 1104, which pertain to the review and amendment of the FSG. Pursuant to these statutory mandates, the United States Sentencing Commission (USSC) in 2004 revised the FSG to ensure their continued effectiveness in deterring organizational misconduct. Notably, the 2004 revisions to the FSG require organizations to "promote an organizational culture that encourages ethical behavior and a commitment to compliance with law."

To understand why this is important for directors, one need only revisit the *Caremark* decision. There, the Delaware Chancery Court opined that "by establishing and maintaining an effective compliance program, board members can protect themselves from personal liability suits." In the wake of that pronouncement, compliance programs that met the "seven elements of effectiveness" outlined by the 1991 FSG quickly became the norm for programs that also met the *Caremark* test for director liability. So, how did the 2004 amendments affect those seven elements? First, and most importantly for directors, the 2004 amendments expressly imposed responsibility for the compliance and ethics program on an organization's "governing authority" (i.e., the board of directors) and its executives. The amendments require that the board of directors be knowledgeable about the content and operation of the compliance program and exercise reasonable oversight of the program.

Additional elements under the 2004 FSG included responsibility by "high-level personnel" within the organization to ensure that the organization's compliance and ethics program is effective; assignment of day-to-day operational responsibility for the program to a designated individual; and allocation of adequate resources and appropriate authority for that individual to carry out responsibility for the program. Additional related requirements under the 2004 amendments included training in ethics and compliance for high-level personnel *and the board*; auditing and monitoring systems intended to detect criminal misconduct; and periodic evaluations of the effectiveness of the compliance and ethics program, which, in

[7] *In re: Citigroup Inc. Shareholder Derivative Litigation*, Del. Ch., Feb. 24, 2009 (Civil Action No. 3338-CC).

reality, require periodic reports to the board by the "high level personnel" in charge of the program.

With the express reaffirmation of *Caremark* by *Stone v. Ritter*, the FSG's 2004 elements of what constitutes an "effective" ethics and compliance program will quickly become, if they have not already become, the gold standard by which ethics and compliance programs and the conduct of directors are judged. Directors would be well advised to heed the Guidelines and treat them as mandatory regulatory requirements.

A month ago (in April 2010), the USSC notably voted to modify the FSG standards for an effective corporate compliance and ethics program.[8] The proposed 2010 amendments include new stress on "responding appropriately" as a mitigating factor in criminal sentencing, and involve such steps as providing restitution, remediating harm to victims, self-reporting, and cooperating with authorities. The 2010 amendments also include a revision to penalty scoring in connection with maintaining an effective compliance program when offenses are committed involving a high-level person (i.e., a senior executive). Under the newest proposed amendment, a company could still receive leniency credit, despite the misconduct of a senior official, by meeting four mandatory criteria in connection with its compliance and ethics program:

- The person or persons with operational responsibility for the ethics and compliance program (the "CECO") must report directly to the board of directors or an appropriate subgroup, such as the audit committee;
- The ethics and compliance program must have uncovered the problem before discovery outside the company was reasonably likely;
- The company must promptly have reported the problem to the government; and,
- No person with operational responsibility for the compliance program participated in, condoned, or was willfully ignorant of the criminal conduct.

These amendments respond to what has been a growing refrain — that the CECO must have the express authority to communicate personally and promptly with the board or an appropriate subgroup of the board (such as the company's audit committee) on any matter involving criminal, or potentially criminal, conduct, and he or she must report on the implementation and effectiveness of the compliance program at least annually.

Although these newly proposed criteria were not added to the formal FSG elements for what constitutes an effective ethics and compliance program, they, like the Thompson/Holder/McNulty memo principles, could be viewed as closely related guidance. By injecting these principles into the FSG, they also potentially become a part of the *Caremark* and *Stone* framework and, by extension, apply to the parameters of board oversight in ensuring that an effective compliance program is in place.

---

[8] See discussion of the originally proposed changes in 75 Fed. Reg. 3525 (March 10, 2010).

Lessons from the Mistakes of Others

As indicated, directors' obligations in this area are constantly evolving, and directors must remain constantly alert for potential changes to the programs that they oversee — particularly as high-profile settlements provide new insights as to what government officials view as "effective" ethics and compliance plans. An examination of several of these settlements shows that, in addition to imposing hundreds of millions of dollars in fines and penalties, enforcement agencies and prosecutors are requiring corporate directors to perform some actions relative to ethics and compliance programs that arguably go beyond mere oversight. Additionally, these settlements (in the form of corporate integrity agreements, deferred prosecution agreements, or consent decrees) often intrude on the directors' otherwise unfettered discretion to manage the corporation by imposing governance and other requirements that otherwise would be the province of the board to decide.

Common themes that run through these settlements are (1) direct reporting by the CECO to the board of directors, (2) certification requirements, (3) required periodic assessments of the ethics and compliance programs, and (4) board and management level compliance committees.

For example, Eli Lilly's CIA provided that the CECO could not report, or be subordinate to, the CFO or the General Counsel. Similar requirements were contained in other such settlements, such as that of AstraZeneca. Eli Lilly was required to have not only a CECO but a Compliance Committee, composed of senior managers of key departments. The agreement recited that the Eli Lilly Board of Directors (or Board Committee composed of independent directors) was responsible for review and oversight of matters related to compliance with federal health care program requirements and the CIA, and further required periodic board/committee review of performance under the company's compliance program, with a copy of each review report to be provided to the OIG. Additionally required were periodic board/committee resolutions summarizing review and oversight of compliance with federal health programs, or, if the board was unable to attest to compliance, reasons why, together with enumeration of steps to resolve. Finally, certain employees, such as the CEO and Vice Presidents involved with marketing and sales, were required to annually certify that their units complied with the CIA, with FDA requirements, and with federal health care program requirements.

Many CIAs require that annual reports submitted to the government include a signed certification from the CECO, personally attesting that the company is in compliance with all aspects of the CIA. An important trend in recent CIAs, however, is the requirement that other company employees and/or members of the board of directors (or committees thereof) also provide corresponding certifications. Board-level certifications were required in the CIAs of companies such as Cephalon, Bayer, and Eli Lilly. The required board certification language was described in each CIA, requiring that the board make a reasonable inquiry into the operations of the company's compliance program and to resolve that, to the best of each board member's knowledge, the company has implemented an effective compliance program. Similarly, a 2009 amendment to the CIA of Aventis added a board-level certification requirement. By requiring board certifications, the government is underscoring that ultimate responsibility for oversight of the company's compliance program lies with the directors. *One might argue that directors already had (or should have had) this responsibility given the interface of traditional fiduciary duties with the FSG; however, the certification requirements in these CIAs unquestionably take the director's responsibilities and potential exposure to a new level.*

A required compliance assessment audit of a company's compliance program is another emerging CIA trend. For example, Bayer's CIA requires that the board retain a compliance expert panel made up of three independent and objective individuals or entities with expertise in compliance with federal health care program and FDA requirements. This panel is required to perform a review of the effectiveness of Bayer's compliance program. Eli Lilly's CIA provided that its compliance committee must "arrange for the performance of a review on the effectiveness of Lilly's Compliance Program for each Reporting Period of the CIA and shall review the results of the Compliance Program Review as part of the review and assessment of Lilly's Compliance Program." Copies of the review were required to be submitted with each of the required annual reports to the OIG. Accordingly, a question that directors must ask in determining the effectiveness of their companies' compliance programs is whether independent compliance audits of the programs should be performed for the purposes of the board level review even prior to coming under the scrutiny of the government through a CIA, Deferred Prosecution Agreement, or Consent Decree.

The Cephalon, Bayer, Eli Lilly, and AstraZeneca CIAs required that either the board or board-level committees provide oversight of their respective compliance programs and meet quarterly to review them. In these CIAs, the board/committee review was required to include, at a minimum, a consideration of the performance of the CECO and the compliance department. The Eli Lilly CIA further specifies that the board committee must be made up of at least three independent directors. This development further demonstrates the government's attempts to place greater responsibility on directors for the effectiveness of the company's compliance program. In considering how to discharge their fiduciary duties in overseeing ethics and compliance programs, directors should consider establishing separate ethics/compliance and risk management committees. When and to the extent necessary, directors also should consider retaining independent third party experts to assist them in their committee roles on these issues.

Finally, an almost universal element of recent CIAs is a provision for the membership and responsibility of each company's management-level compliance committee. The language is substantially similar for each: "The Compliance Committee shall, at a minimum, include the Chief Compliance Officer and other members of senior management necessary to meet the requirements of this CIA." In addition, these CIAs provide specific examples of personnel and/or departments that should be included in the management-level compliance committee. Examples, in most cases, include the CEO and members from the following departments: legal, human resources, marketing, business development, operations, finance, and sales. The lesson here for directors of companies simply trying to oversee the effectiveness of their companies' ethics and compliance program is to determine whether a management committee should be established and, if so, who should make up its members. A benefit to broad participation is that ethics and compliance becomes the responsibility of the entire company, rather than just the compliance department. Companies should ensure that relevant departments and/or personnel have ownership in compliance-related activities (e.g., policy and procedure development, monitoring activities). In this way, the "seven elements of compliance" become embedded throughout the organization.

Observations and Tips for Directors

Recent trends in law and enforcement activity merely reinforce what most directors already knew: After Enron and Sarbanes-Oxley, it is more important than ever for directors to act diligently, to avoid any appearance of conflict of interest, to assure themselves that they are fully apprised of all material facts surrounding a proposed decision, to ask questions of management, to make a record of their involvement, and to ensure that they obtain appropriate advice from independent experts.

The Sarbanes-Oxley Act clearly resulted in a shift in the balance of power between boards and management. Nevertheless, and despite the heightened levels of board responsibility, skepticism remains today about the effectiveness of board oversight. As two commentators notably said in 2003, "[i]t is far from certain ... how much better public companies govern themselves [now] than they did before the [Sarbanes-Oxley] reforms."[9]

In principle, the shift in power toward boards should embolden directors to "seize the moment." Public officials, such as former SEC Chairman William Donaldson, have called on corporate America to put honesty and integrity at the heart of every business decision. Consonant with the standards of the FSG and recent agency pronouncements, the board oversight obligation for compliance and ethics emerges as something that goes way beyond "checking the box." Rather, it is a call for regular, hands-on review of the health and status of the company's compliance and ethics program, and for review of significant matters raised through direct reports from the CECO. Failure by the board to fulfill these responsibilities may undercut compliance mechanisms within the firm and places the directors at risk for liability in the event of scandal.

With this in mind, directors should consider the following tips when approaching issues associated with ethics or ethics and compliance programs:

- Ensure that the corporation has and maintains a high standard of integrity and ethical conduct. After Enron and the host of other corporate scandals of the past few years, smart directors know that an honest and transparent culture is the best safeguard of

[9] C. Hymowitz and J. Lublin, "Scandals Prompted Changes, But Critics Say More Are Needed to Prevent Another Enron," *Wall Street Journal* (July 22, 2003).

shareholder value and, consequently, the best protection for directors. This begins with "tone at the top."

- Understand that good corporate governance is more than about "checking the box." Process counts. The fact that Disney's directors spent ten years in litigation underscores the importance of a robust process for approving important business decisions. On "checking the box," recall that Enron had an award-winning 62-page code of conduct.
- Make time on the board agenda for periodic training and education to ensure directors are well versed on their oversight obligations for the company's ethics and compliance activities and are prepared to ask the right questions of senior management and the CECO. Direct, unfiltered reports from the CECO are a must. A good closing question to the CECO at every executive session could be, "What else should we be asking?" "Is there anything else we should know?" or "If you were me, what questions would you be asking? "
- Identify the highest compliance and ethics risks of the company and how the compliance and ethics program is addressing these risks. Be prepared to ask tough questions, including, "How is management embedding the program into the operations of the company?" And, "How do the company's mitigating measures stack up against peer companies and industry best practice?"
- Ensure that audit committees get periodic reports of "whistleblower" calls and significant litigation and claims. The emphasis on whistleblower protection under Sarbanes-Oxley reflects the overwhelming importance of whistleblowers in the detection of fraud — and in turn, the importance of strong compliance mechanisms to ensure that material whistleblower concerns really do reach the board.
- In line with recent agency pronouncements and the FSG, ensure that the company conducts a periodic assessment of its compliance and ethics program by an independent, qualified expert.
- Ensure that the minutes of board and committee meetings reflect a deliberative process and the appropriate resolution of matters. Appropriate minutes-taking by a skilled professional can help to minimize litigation risks for directors. The Disney directors notably spent 10 years in litigation and 37 days in trial establishing what a good set of minutes could have established very easily. The lesson for boards is crystal clear.
- Recognize that the basics of board practice still matter and that new compliance structures do not replace judgment. Directors should insist on receiving materials well in advance of board meetings, meetings should be scheduled so as to provide sufficient time for deliberations, and draft minutes should be circulated promptly after the conclusion of meetings. The key for directors, in guarding against liability, is to carefully exercise informed business judgment, including as to ethics and compliance matters.

- Remain vigilant! Rapid evolution of law and enforcement standards pertaining to board oversight of compliance and ethics complicates the directors' role. In consequence, the best safeguard to liability is continuing attention to new precedents, regulatory pronouncements, sentencing standards, etc.

CORPORATE COUNSEL PERSPECTIVE: THE CRISIS OF ETHICS AND THE NEED FOR A COMPLIANCE-SAVVY BOARD

John P. Hansen, *Center for Business Ethics, Bentley University; Compliance and Ethics Committee, Association of Corporate Counsel*

Remarks presented on May 12, 2010

As we (hopefully) begin to emerge from the economic crisis of the past couple of years, I'm reminded of the quip attributed to Stanford economist Paul Romer: "A crisis is a terrible thing to waste." There is much to be learned from the circumstances that contributed to the financial debacle and related business scandals of recent years. Those of us who labor in the compliance and ethics field or are thought leaders in governance and ethics can benefit from an examination of this recent history.

There is substantial evidence that on compliance and ethics issues — the foundation for fostering accountability and trust in business integrity — companies are not doing a good enough job. According to the World Economic Forum, more than two-thirds of people globally believe the current economic crisis is a crisis of ethics and values.[1] Other survey data confirms substantial skepticism about public trust in business.[2]

Ethics and compliance are essential to responsible corporate behavior. Despite substantial efforts in creating the infrastructure, there is something missing in the way many businesses today fulfill their ethics and compliance mission. In the quest to foster responsible corporate behavior, and regain the trust that has been lost, companies — especially boards and in-house counsel — need to examine present practices. We have some work to do.

Detecting a Pulse

Late last year, the Compliance and Ethics Committee of the Association of Corporate Counsel[3] undertook a survey of the association's membership. Our goal was to take the pulse of the in-house legal community to learn what corporate counsel are actually doing in the areas of compliance and ethics within their organizations. The data suggest that there is substantial room for improvement. Based on over 1600 responding lawyers:

- Only half of the survey respondents reported that their organizations assess in any way whether they operate ethically; and more broadly, just over a third reported that they have a mechanism for assessing whether their organizations operate responsibly.

---

[1] Full report available at: http://www.weforum.org/pdf/faith/valuesreport.pdf

[2] See www.edelman.com/trust/2010/

[3] The Association of Corporate Counsel (ACC) is the world's largest association of in-house counsel representing over 26,000 members working in over 10,000 public, private, and non-profit organizations in more than 70 countries.

- Only half of the respondents reported providing their boards with compliance or ethics training.
- 78% reported that their organizations never or only rarely undertake ethics risk assessments.

These data may help to explain the public's jaded perception of the state of ethics in business. It is a perception that has been made acute in the aftermath of the financial collapse, which has been called a betrayal of public trust.[4] This paper does not presume to serve as a detailed analysis of the governance deficiencies associated with the financial crisis. Nevertheless, the crisis is arguably a powerful indicator of the inadequacies associated with compliance and ethics as practiced in many companies, and perhaps especially so in financial services firms, which ironically are widely considered to have some of the most substantial risk and compliance infrastructures.

<u>When Ethical Shortcuts Become a Business Norm</u>

As a longtime financial services executive, Ken Costa is someone whose insights are worth noting. The chairman of Lazard International has written and commented on the extent and scope of the breaches of trust associated with the mortgage meltdown. He identifies the first betrayal as what occurred between individual subprime borrowers and banks. Lenders essentially suspended responsible underwriting because they had no plans to carry the loans on their books. The subprime market introduced a new brand of financial product, so-called "liar's loans" or "NINJA loans" — "no income, no job or assets." Economists call this "moral hazard." It could also be called the initial stage of a crisis in the making.

Costa points out that the breaches of trust didn't end there.

A second betrayal occurred in the development and marketing of mortgage-backed securities, particularly in the exchange of information between ratings agencies and banks. The conflict of interest inherent in having ratings firms paid by issuers is best illustrated in the email from a Moody's analyst in which he described the practice of assigning AAA ratings to mortgage-backed securities as having "sold our soul to the devil for revenue."[5]

The third betrayal is evident in the design of compensation schemes with perverse incentives. This includes Countrywide CEO Angelo Mozilo's mega-million dollar compensation package, as well as the comparatively modest but still poorly structured compensation arrangements by which mortgage brokers and even home appraisers were paid in ways and in amounts that knowingly encouraged irresponsible business practices.

---

[4] Speech by Kenneth Costa: "Of the People for the People: Re-building the trust economy." Delivered on September 24, 2009; available at www.gresham.ac.uk/event.asp?PageId=45&EventId=100

[5] Bloomberg.com, 10/22/2008; available at http://www.bloomberg.com/apps/news?pid=20670001&sid=aF7PmyInpu7c

And, finally, the fourth betrayal is seen in the fact that the risk of failure was nationalized, while the rewards of success were privatized. More than any other factor, this contributed to public frustration and anger — and fueled public skepticism about the trustworthiness of business.

These betrayals did not come about from the likes of a rogue like Bernie Madoff; instead, they emerged from routine business practices carried out by leading firms. The corporate players involved in creating the crisis — Countrywide Financial, Moody's, and Lehman Brothers among many others — were exemplars of capitalist enterprise. Yet at every crossroad, entire industries displayed an abject failure of accountability and fiduciary responsibility.

We need to better understand how these circumstances came to pass and, more importantly, what they portend about the inadequacies in the design and operation of compliance and ethics programs, including board oversight.

Boards and Lawyers: Two Pillars for Compliance and Ethics

There is substantial variability in the design and operation of corporate compliance and ethics programs, as well as the governance structure for board oversight. A practice seen in many organizations is for the compliance and ethics role to be integrated with the legal officer role.[6] Even when this is not the case — and there may be an emerging trend away from doing so — in-house counsel have significant responsibility for compliance and ethics matters, whether as a manager of the program or as a key subject-matter expert and resource to a separate compliance function.

At the apex of the organizational hierarchy sits the board of directors. Entrusted with the fiduciary duty to serve shareholder (and arguably stakeholder) interests and to act as a check upon management, board members are heavily dependent on the expertise of their advisors in carrying out their oversight responsibilities. On matters of compliance and ethics, unless there is an independent compliance and ethics officer charged with this responsibility, it is typically the general counsel who reports to the board on such matters.

We need to examine whether the framework for compliance and ethics governance — at least as it is practiced today — is adequate to the task we place upon it. All too often, "ethics" in business is presented as a saccharine platitude rather than a serious measure of corporate and individual performance.

The Elephant in the Room

Although compliance and ethics programs are designed to help mitigate certain risks, ironically there is one particular risk that compliance and ethics programs can actually create. It is the risk of complacency — the notion that "we've got that base covered."

---

[6] According to a recent Association of Corporate Counsel and Corpedia report, 37% of individuals surveyed report that their organization maintains a combined position.

In practice, compliance and ethics programs too easily can be mere illusions — a veritable Potemkin village of corporate rectitude. Codes of conduct, computer-based training for employees, posters displaying the reporting hotline — each element is a technical measure of good practice. In total, however, do they produce an ethical (or even legally compliant) organization? Probably not.

Each of the participants in the subprime mortgage scandal could demonstrate the existence of a compliance and ethics program, including oversight by a committee of the board. Why, then, were there such fundamental failures with respect to the most basic risk issues, not to mention ethical vulnerabilities inherent in routine business practices?

The answer in part may lie in the design and operation of many compliance and ethics programs. While each of the elements prescribed by the Federal Organizational Sentencing Guidelines may be present in at least a rudimentary form — thus permitting "checking the box" — what is often lacking is a meaningful commitment to accountability, transparency, responsibility, and actual implementation. The guidelines recognize this potential shortcoming and thus in 2004 adopted the language about the need to create a culture of compliance and ethics.

Ironically, the prevalent practice of having legal counsel advise the board on "compliance and ethics" may tend to present an excessively legalistic approach to the topic, which can obscure other relevant considerations such as, for example, the cultural influences that impact employee behaviors or the nuances that distinguish between a "paper program" (i.e., one that merely looks impressive on paper) and one that actually drives desired behavior in a meaningful way. This is not to suggest that lawyers as a body are unable or unwilling to understand compliance and ethics in its most fulsome form — simply that in many cases we have seen, that does not happen. Clearly, legal counsel has an immediate obligation to ensure that their firms meet the minimum threshold requirements for compliance under the law; but too often, a focus on minimal compliance requirements can obscure a longer-range vision for inculcating ethical principles and culture within the firm.

Do boards understand the difference between checking the box and a fully robust, implemented and effective program? Do they have a working knowledge of what constitutes best practice in their industry, or the probing questions they should be asking their CEO, ethics and compliance officers, the general counsel, and other senior management? Do they have a plan for how to address legal and ethical concerns that rise through the employee hotline or other channels to the top? It is possible that many do not. As shown by our committee's survey, many boards do not receive education and training, despite the fact that it is a practice expressly contemplated by the Federal Sentencing Guidelines.[7]

---

[7] See §8B2.1, Federal Sentencing Guidelines; available at http://www.ussc.gov/2007guid/8b2_1.html

We need to better understand what is working — or not working — in compliance and ethics programs, including the efficacy of board oversight. As part of this self-assessment, boards should develop a keener understanding of not just the baseline elements of an effective compliance and ethics program according to the Federal Sentencing Guidelines, but what the emerging "best practices" are in this highly dynamic and evolving area. Further, boards need to have a structure for ensuring that important matters in key risk areas rise to their attention, and the right competencies within their ranks to address them efficiently and effectively.

A Confluence of Thought Leadership

A recent Blue Ribbon Commission report issued by the National Association of Corporate Directors (NACD)[8] highlights the critical role of board responsibility in risk governance. Ethics and compliance are integrally related to risk governance, and therefore the principles of effective risk oversight identified in the report are germane to our discussion. Of particular note are the following:

- Consider whether the company's risk management system — including people and processes — is appropriate and has sufficient resources.[9]
- Work with management to understand and agree on the types (and format) of risk information the board requires.[10]
- Encourage a dynamic and constructive risk dialogue between management and the board, including a willingness to challenge assumptions.[11]
- Closely monitor the potential risks in the company's culture and its incentive structure. How does senior management demonstrate its commitment to an appropriate corporate culture?[12]
- Assess the board's risk oversight processes and include necessary board education and training regarding risk.[13]

Each of these principles has direct relevance to a company's compliance and ethics function. Meaningful oversight implies active engagement, which is more than mere "review and concur." If followed, these principles can help inform not just board oversight, but the way in which a company actually designs and carries out its compliance and ethics practices.

---

[8] Report of the NACD Blue Ribbon Commission on Risk Governance: Balancing Risk and Reward (2009).

[9] *Id.* at 15.

[10] *Id.*

[11] *Id.* at 16.

[12] *Id.* at 17.

[13] *Id.* at 18–19.

A complementary set of principles was laid out in a 2009 Conference Board report titled *Ethics and the Board*,[14] which asserted that oversight of business integrity is a fundamental part of directors' responsibility for their firms' reputational capital. Consonant with the foregoing, the Conference Board notably suggested that effective enterprise risk management (ERM) is closely tied into compliance and ethics oversight and, in consequence, that directors should demand a "high level of cross-functional collaboration on issues of business integrity" from management.[15] The Conference Board also enunciated other steps for boards to take in fulfilling their compliance and ethics role:

- Factor business integrity issues into the selection of new board members.[16]
- Put "teeth" into incentive structures for management, aligned with promoting performance with integrity.[17]
- Ensure that the compliance and ethics function within firms is properly resourced and empowered.[18]
- Seek out appropriate information, advice, and guidance on business integrity issues, both from within management and from the outside.[19]

Another worthy contribution to the literature on governance and business integrity is the recent Policy Brief issued by the Committee for Economic Development.[20] Spearheaded by Ben W. Heineman, Jr., former GE Senior Vice President for Law and Public Affairs, this white paper identifies as the "first task" the need to redefine the corporate mission away from short-term maximization of shareholder value and towards reinforcing objectives that include a commitment to integrity. The report also identifies the need to re-align board oversight to track the highest priority performance, risk, and integrity issues. In both instances, the primacy of integrity is recognized as fundamental to the corporate mission. In turn, a well-designed compliance and ethics program overseen by a well-informed and engaged board can be instrumental in helping to restore trust in corporate governance.

Achieving these aims will require active collaboration between board members, in-house counsel, and compliance and ethics managers within the firm, with the goal of achieving a compliance-savvy board. The impetus to that collaboration, however, may require that we admit the obvious: For many organizations today, compliance and ethics is a "check the box"

---

[14] The Conference Board, Ethics and the Board: Integrating Integrity into Business Strategy (2009).
[15] *Id.* at 16.
[16] *Id.* at 15.
[17] *Id.* at 17.
[18] *Id.* at 17–18.
[19] *Id.* at 19.
[20] Committee for Economic Development, *Restoring Trust in Corporate Governance: The Six Essential Tasks of Boards of Directors and Business Leaders* (2010); available at http://www.ced.org/images/library/reports/corporate_governance/cgPolicyBrief0110.pdf

exercise that especially tends to shortchange the notion of a robust approach to integrity. That needs to change.

Creating a Compliance-Savvy Board

Not all governance changes require Sarbanes-Oxley–like time and expense. In-house counsel and board members can work to create more effective compliance and ethics systems in their companies by considering and acting on several key issues:

- *Appropriate organizational placement of the compliance and ethics function.* Where the organization places the compliance and ethics function is a critical governance issue that requires thoughtful consideration. An informed decision to place this role within the General Counsel's office requires an objective assessment of the pros and cons of doing so.[21] Boards should ask such questions as: How does placement of the compliance and ethics role within the Legal Department impact the effectiveness of the function? Is there a potential conflict between the respective roles of law, compliance, and ethics and, if so, how does management intend to manage those tensions? Alternatively, Should the compliance and ethics function stand independently from the legal group? While law, compliance, and ethics ideally complement and reinforce one another, it is important to recognize that this may not always be the case. Is the board satisfied with management's ability to fulfill disparate responsibilities if the roles are structurally merged?[22]
- *Unfiltered access to the board by the individual with day-to-day operational responsibility for ethics and compliance.* New attention is being focused on this issue as the FSG have now been expressly revised to highlight the importance of unfettered access by the individual with the clearest line of operational vision (from the trenches) to those who need to know (i.e., the board in its oversight role). Boards are entitled to straightforward reporting that is not subjected to prior review, approval, or excessive

---

[21] For a consideration of some of the arguments in support of or against general counsel oversight of the ethics and compliance function, see *The Ethics and Compliance Handbook: A Practical Guide from Leading Organizations* (Waltham, MA: Ethics and Compliance Officer Association Foundation , 2008), p. 37.

[22] For fuller consideration of this important issue, two seminal resources are *Leading Corporate Integrity: Defining the Role of the Chief Ethics & Compliance Officer (CECO)* (Washington, D.C.: Ethics Resource Center, 2007); available at http://www.ethics.org/resource/ceco; and Donna C. Boehme, "From Enron to Madoff: Why Many Corporate Compliance and Ethics Programs Are Positioned for Failure" (Arlington, VA: RAND Corporation, 2009); available at http://www.rand.org/pubs/conf_proceedings/2009/RAND_CF258.pdf. In addition, it is instructive that the healthcare sector makes a particularly strong case for segregating the compliance and ethics function from the legal function. See, e.g., "Corporate Integrity Agreement between Pfizer Inc. and Office of Inspector General of the Department of Health and Human Services" (2009); available at http://oig.hhs.gov/fraud/cia/agreements/pfizer_inc_08312009.pdf

editing by intervening management. *When such review is performed by well-intentioned in-house counsel, it can result in reporting that is filtered through a highly legal lens that can miss important matters, such as emerging ethics risks. Direct access to* the board by the individual with day-to-day operational responsibility and *oversight by* the board are corollaries. The former cannot be abridged without compromising the latter.

- *The influence of organizational culture on business conduct.* Organizational culture reflects what companies and employees in fact *do* as opposed to what they might *say* they do. Does the company seek to measure and understand these influences (through employee surveys, focus groups, or other methods)? It is doubtful whether effective oversight of an ethics and compliance program could take place in the absence of a critical assessment on the part of the board of management's efforts at fostering the right set of cultural values and norms. Evaluating program effectiveness, in fact, is one of the elements prescribed by the Federal Sentencing Guidelines.[23] A related issue is whether the assessment should be performed by internal resources or external experts.[24] The decision should follow collaboration among the board and management. In either case, the assessment itself should be carried out by persons who are not responsible for managing the compliance and ethics program.
- *The relevance of "ethics" in risk assessments.* There is an all-too-frequent propensity in business to gloss over the significance of the term "ethics." The term has a profoundly different meaning than "compliance." If the organization aspires to deliver on its commitment to creating a culture of ethics and compliance, then it should give appropriate consideration to the ethical implications of business decisions. Based on our committee survey, however, it does not appear that "ethics" receives much consideration despite the fact it is a powerful internal control that warrants appropriate attention at every level of decision-making. It is interesting to speculate whether an ethics risk assessment by the financial services firms involved in subprime lending might have led to a different outcome.
- *Meaningful board reporting and instructive board education.* As boards have greater demands thrust upon them, it is all the more critical to ensure that the board's energies are focused properly on the key issues. This presents two distinct yet related issues: the need for reports to the board that are relevant, informative, and can lead to active discussion (as opposed to passive listening), and the need for appropriate board education. Reporting and training are separate concepts, so why are they discussed here together? Simply put, it appears that many boards are not well informed about how to perform their oversight responsibilities with respect to compliance and ethics. They often do not know the right questions to ask (including

[23] See §8B2.1(b)(5) Federal Sentencing Guidelines.

[24] For a discussion about the various "pros" and "cons" of external evaluations, see *The Ethics and Compliance Handbook: A Practical Guide From Leading Organizations*, p. 159.

some that are implied in the earlier bullets noted above, such as, for example, the importance of unfiltered access). Boards need to acquire a deeper understanding of the unique role they have with respect to overseeing the compliance and ethics function. Not unlike the need to ensure financial and accounting expertise among members of the audit committee, board members responsible for overseeing compliance and ethics management should possess (or acquire) appropriate expertise in this area. Among the topical areas implied by such expertise are (i) understanding of the role, responsibilities, and risks of board oversight; (ii) actual oversight of program implementation and effectiveness; and (iii) substantive knowledge of program content and operation.[25]

Creating a compliance-savvy board is essential if we are to ensure robust compliance and ethics programs that are more than Potemkin villages. While programs themselves are not a panacea for the sort of systemic failures we have observed of late, they do represent a framework by which companies can work to ensure more accountable enterprises sustained by responsible business conduct. As stewards of our free enterprise system, those of us who are thought leaders in the governance, compliance, and ethics community share a responsibility to foster such efforts. As we emerge from the throes of an economic crisis, there is an opportunity to rebuild a foundation of trust in our business organizations. It is an opportunity we must not waste.

---

[25] For an elaboration on evolving standards of board training and reporting issues, see Donna C. Boehme, "Not Your Father's Board Training — What Today's Boards Need to Know About Ethics and Compliance," webinar delivered February 18, 2010; available at http://www.ethicspoint.com/event/not-your-fathers-board-training---what-todays-boards-need-to-know-about-ethics-and-compliance.

BOARD OVERSIGHT OF COMPLIANCE, ETHICS, INTEGRITY, AND REPUTATION RISKS: WHAT DIRECTORS NEED TO KNOW

Keith T. Darcy, *Ethics & Compliance Officer Association*
Remarks presented on May 12, 2010

The financial crisis of 2007–2008 set off an economic tsunami that brought world economies to their knees. The Great Recession resulted in trillions of dollars in lost consumer wealth, record foreclosures and personal bankruptcies, double digit unemployment in the United States, and the collapse of major financial institutions and of key manufacturing businesses.

There are no simple explanations for the meltdown. Clearly, innovation in financial products resulted in the proliferation of increasingly complex financial instruments (mortgage-backed securities, CDOs, CDSs, etc.), the risks of which were not well understood, even within the financial services industry. Financial complexity and lack of insight into risk, combined with excessive leverage and widespread fraudulent practices within the U.S. home mortgage sector, left many financial institutions vulnerable. As we know now in hindsight, these conditions created the potential for cascading credit defaults and failures among financial institutions. Unfortunately, regulation did not keep up with a rapidly changing marketplace. Financial innovation, along with inadequate regulatory oversight, is clearly a recipe for disaster.

While Wall Street bears a large share of responsibility for the meltdown, this crisis has many culprits. Gatekeepers everywhere — including corporate boards, regulators, rating agencies, internal and external auditors — failed to recognize certain fraudulent practices and to understand the risks of complex transactions. In retrospect, these various watchdogs overlooked obvious signs of conflicts-of-interest, preferential treatment, executive excess, and a culture of greed. Today directors of many large financial institutions and industrial corporations are being criticized and subjected to regulatory and shareholder scrutiny over corporate failures that led to our economic collapse.

As a result of this crisis, the U.S. is undergoing an unprecedented wave of corporate governance and regulatory reforms. As I discuss below, promulgations by regulators, Congress, and the White House are placing new demands on the way corporations are governed. How will these new issues be managed? Are boards prepared and sufficiently informed to step up to heightened expectations, particularly with regard to ethics and compliance oversight for their firms? Will boards necessarily involve their chief ethics and compliance officers as a key resource for meeting the new expectations? And will the increasing and changing requirements for boards, particularly regarding ethics and compliance, ultimately result in reduced risks to the organization?

Federal Sentencing Guidelines and SOX on the Responsibility of Boards for C&E

Clearly, the board has substantial responsibilities as the guardian of the firm. In addition to ensuring that the firm's business is conducted with a sound strategy and prudence, good governance requires that directors protect shareholders' assets, including the firm's reputation. The fiduciary obligations of the board concerning ethics and compliance programs have been made clear by the Federal Sentencing Guidelines (FSG) and include, among other things:

- That the board must be knowledgeable about the content and operation of the firm's compliance and ethics program;
- That the board must reasonably oversee the implementation and effectiveness of the program;
- That there must be a high-level person charged with oversight for the program;
- That the individual with operational responsibility for the program must have adequate resources and appropriate authority to execute her/his responsibilities;
- That this individual must have direct, unfiltered access to the board;[1]
- That the firm must take reasonable steps to communicate appropriate behaviors and conduct effective training for all individuals, including the board.

The oversight responsibilities of the board are also informed by several major provisions under the Sarbanes-Oxley Act of 2002 (SOX).[2] SOX introduced new standards of accountability for directors of U.S. public companies, including companies listed on U.S. stock exchanges. For example, under Section 406 of SOX, public companies must either: (1) institute a formal code of conduct for senior financial officers to promote *"honest and ethical conduct, including the ethical handling of actual or apparent conflicts-of-interest between personal and professional relationships…fair, accurate and timely disclosure…and compliance with applicable rules and regulations"* or else (2) disclose the reasons for neglecting to adopt such a code. In a different vein, Section 806 of SOX provides protection to whistleblowers by prohibiting discrimination in the terms of employment or other forms of harassment against those who blow the whistle internally on certain types of misconduct.

---

[1] Note that both the 2004 and 2010 FSG amendments contemplate that the person with day-to-day operational responsibility for the compliance and ethics program will have direct access to the governing authority of the company (i.e., the board). The 2010 amendments further create an incentive for companies to ensure that that person *"has express authority to communicate personally to the governing authority or appropriate subgroup thereof (A) promptly on any matter involving criminal conduct or potential criminal conduct, and (B) no less than annually on the implementation and effectiveness of the compliance and ethics program."* See U.S. Sentencing Commission (April 30, 2010), *Amendments to the Sentencing Guidelines, Policy Statements and Commentary*, at 18. Available online at http://www.ussc.gov/2010guid/finalamend10.pdf

[2] The Sarbanes–Oxley Act of 2002 (Pub.L. 107-204, 116 Stat. 745, enacted July 30, 2002).

Perhaps most important under SOX Section 404, the establishment of adequate internal controls is underlined as a direct responsibility for management and the directors. By extension, the failure to establish adequate controls presumably bears significant personal risks for the directors.

The CECO as a Key Resource for Directors on C&E Matters

Given the many internal and external issues potentially impacting a company's reputation, how can a corporate director protect shareholders' assets through compliance and ethics oversight? More specifically, how can directors minimize a company's ethical liabilities and maximize its ethical assets? And what is the appropriate role of the board in setting and overseeing a tone of ethical leadership for the firm? As the Federal Sentencing Guidelines implicitly recognize, a central element of the board's role involves its relationship to a chief ethics and compliance officer (CECO), an executive with day-to-day oversight responsibility for ethics and compliance matters within the firm.[3] Clearly, many other key executives have responsibilities to inform and assist the board in the discharge of specific aspects of its fiduciary duties, such as the CEO, CFO, director of human resources, and internal auditor. It follows that, in the critical area of compliance, integrity, and culture issues, the CECO is similarly the principal agent for the directors in meeting their regulatory and extra-regulatory responsibilities.

In order for the CECO to serve as an effective resource to support the directors in the discharge of their responsibilities, it is essential that the CECO be an executive level officer with reporting responsibilities both to the CEO and the board. He or she must be involved in the day-to-day strategic, operating, and policy decisions of the firm in order effectively to manage reputation and integrity risks. This kind of responsibility follows from the functions that the CECO is expected to perform, particularly in overseeing the conduct of other top executives, and in driving an ethics and compliance agenda at all levels of the firm.[4]

---

[3] See U.S. Sentencing Commission, *Guidelines Manual*, §8B2.1 (Nov. 2009), available online at http://www.ussc.gov/2009guid/TABCON09.htm

[4] For a further discussion of the critical role of an empowered, senior-level, experienced CECO, see Donna C. Boehme, "From Enron to Madoff: Why Many Corporate Compliance and Ethics Programs Are Positioned for Failure," in Greenberg, *Perspectives of Chief Ethics and Compliance Officers on the Detection and Prevention of Corporate Misdeeds: What the Policy Community Should Know*, Santa Monica, CA: RAND Corporation, CF-258-RC (2009). Available online at http://www.rand.org/pubs/conf_proceedings/2009/RAND_CF258.pdf. See also Ethics Resource Center (2008), *Leading Corporate Integrity: Defining the Role of the Chief Ethics and Compliance Officer (CECO)*. Available online at http://www.ethics.org/files/u5/CECO_Paper_UPDATED.pdf. Per the latter, *"[E]thical considerations are present in many business-related decisions ranging from performance standards for merit increases to reduction of head count or integration of new organizational cultures through mergers and acquisitions. On a daily basis, senior executives make decisions that affect many people and therefore have an ethical component. For this reason, the CECO should be considered a member of the senior executive team." Id.* at 24.

In a related vein, recent corporate scandals bear evidence that senior executives like the CEO, CFO, general counsel, and other top officers are most likely to show up in the reports of the Department of Justice Corporate Fraud Task Force. Appropriate placement and resourcing of the CECO are critical to that person being able to detect and intervene in episodes of senior executive misconduct —and by corollary, to enable the board to detect and intervene as well.[5]

By contrast, a lower level employee in the CECO role is not likely to have the clout to intervene at the senior executive level, let alone influence decisions being made in the C suite. The CECO must be a part of the company's executive power structure if she is to be effective in this way. Only the board can give that authority and assurance to the CECO, and in turn, only through the CECO can the board fulfill its oversight responsibilities here.

Independence of the CECO is critical to effective performance in many aspects of his or her role, and unfiltered access to the board is merely the first step in assuring this. Absent independence, the CECO may become vulnerable to pressure from other executives in connection with ethically questionable or illegal practices — a result that undercuts the role of the CECO and that potentially puts the board at risk, as well. In support of greater independence for the CECO, some companies structure the position so that the board directly hires and fires the CECO, determines the CECO's compensation and benefits, and frames the scope of the CECO's management responsibilities. CECO independence can be further assured by providing an employment contract, ample severance, indemnification, and full D&O insurance coverage.[6]

Board-backed independence for the CECO can ensure that she has the appropriate authority to carry out her mandate and, by extension, to help fulfill the responsibilities of the board for C&E oversight as well.

---

[5] For relevant background on prosecutions of senior executives by the Department of Justice Corporate Fraud Task Force, see U.S. Department of Justice (July 17, 2007), *Fact Sheet: President's Corporate Fraud Task Force Marks Five Years of Ensuring Corporate Integrity*, available online at http://www.justice.gov/opa/pr/2007/July/07_odag_507.html. In 2007, the Corporate Fraud Task Force marked its 5-year anniversary by announcing a total of 1,236 corporate fraud convictions then to date, including 214 chief executive officers and presidents, 53 chief financial officers, 23 corporate counsels or attorneys, and 129 vice presidents. See *id.*

[6] On this point, the Ethics Resource Center observed that CECOs frequently "occupy a delicate position, especially if ... wrongdoing ... takes place among executive management. Regardless of the reporting relationship, a CECO should be hired only upon review and approval by the board.... Similarly, the CECO should not be terminated unless review ... by the board has taken place. Doing so ... helps to protect the CECO from retaliation by peers or ... senior management." See Ethics Resource Center (2008), Leading Corporate Integrity: Defining the Role of the Chief Ethics and Compliance Officer (CECO). Available online at http://www.ethics.org/files/u5/CECO_Paper_UPDATED.pdf

Expanding Board Responsibilities Make the CECO Role Even More Critical

Today, the responsibilities and risks for fiduciaries of listed companies are clearly expanding. In December 2009, the Securities and Exchange Commission (SEC) adopted several major disclosure changes which fall into two major categories, compensation and governance.[7]

Regarding compensation, boards must now disclose the broader pay policies of the corporation, and not just for named executive officers. Disclosure requirements are triggered: (1) where compensation policies bear potentially greater organizational risks, (2) where compensation systems are noticeably different across the organization, (3) where operating units are significantly more profitable, or (4) where compensation is a significant percentage of revenue. In addition, there are new required disclosures regarding relationships and fees with compensation consultants. SEC filings this spring will bear first witness to how companies address these new requirements.

The SEC is also requiring new disclosures regarding governance. This includes new evidence of directors' backgrounds, experiences, skills, industry knowledge, and, therefore, why they are qualified to serve as fiduciaries. In addition, and very importantly, the regulator is now requiring additional disclosure on the board's role in risk management, including how the board sets parameters for risk to the organization. In this context, it will be interesting to see how many companies regard their CECOs as part of the senior risk management team.

The SEC is also asking companies to disclose how the board addresses director-level diversity, without providing guidance or a definition for "diversity." Lastly, boards will now be required to disclose the processes and resources they use to identify climate change issues. This includes how fiduciaries receive information on greenhouse emissions, the reliability of that information, how institutional responsibility is assigned to oversee and implement climate change policies, and how executives are held accountable and rewarded.

Beyond these regulatory changes, Congress has also been considering legislative action that would further impact the board role. For example, the Shareholder Bill of Rights Act recently brought forward by Senator Charles Schumer (New York) and Congressman Gary Peter (Michigan) is aimed at curbing excessive risk-taking and runaway compensation.[8] That bill, if passed, would: (1) open shareholder proxy access, (2) end staggered boards, (3) create widespread "say-on-pay" votes, and (4) create separate "risk" committees of boards for independent directors while requiring a risk expert on the board of directors. And of course, the Restoring American Financial Stability Act proposed by Senator Chris Dodd (Connecticut),

---

[7] For background and commentary on the new SEC rules, see U.S. Securities and Exchange Commission (December 16, 2009), *SEC Approves Enhanced Disclosure About Risk, Compensation and Corporate Governance*, available online at http://www.sec.gov/news/press/2009/2009-268.htm. See also U.S. Securities and Exchange Commission, "Proxy Disclosure Enhancements: Final Rule," 74 *Fed. Reg.* 68334 (December 23, 2009).

[8] The Shareholder Bill of Rights Act of 2009, S.1074.

currently being debated in the Senate, would also make significant changes in current corporate governance practices along similar lines.[9]

Even the White House has gotten involved in corporate governance matters, by causing the termination of GM's CEO and through the appointment of "pay czar" Ken Feinberg to oversee compensation for TARP-funded companies. And in a somewhat less overt action, the administration appears to be gearing up for stronger enforcement activity, as reflected by increased budget appropriations by 13% at the SEC and 23% at DOJ.

Taken together, these various rules, proposals, and policies suggest a massive new wave of corporate governance regulation and enforcement, with concomitant risks for firms and their boards. To be effective in overseeing compliance with these new requirements, boards will minimally need: (1) knowledge of applicable standards and (2) an empowered CECO. In addition, directors should:

- Understand the risks they face as fiduciaries and how these can be mitigated or resolved;
- Recognize and fulfill their responsibilities to oversee the company's management of compliance, ethics, and reputation risks;
- Ensure the board agenda includes periodic training on matters of compliance and ethics, including what constitutes an effective program and industry best practice;
- Make time on the board agenda, and especially in executive session, for periodic progress reports from the CECO;
- Receive briefings on the highest compliance and ethics risks for the company and what the company is doing to mitigate them;
- Make certain the CECO (the person tasked with day-to-day operational management of the program) is an empowered member of senior management with direct, unfiltered access to the board.

Conclusion

The "Great Recession" has harmed virtually every citizen and caused extraordinary economic and social dislocation. In 2008 and 2009, trillions of dollars of taxpayer money was employed to offset frozen credit markets, as well as lack of consumer spending and business investment. In the process, consumer rage boiled over, bringing down the wrath of Congress and government regulators on those who breached the public trust. As a result, reputational risk for firms today is at least as great as strategic, operating, and financial risk. A rumor or hint of malfeasance or disregard for the law, and the market value of the franchise is at risk — as illustrated only too well by the recent indictment brought by the SEC against Goldman Sachs. As fiduciaries, corporate directors bear great responsibilities to bring wisdom to the

[9] The Restoring American Financial Stability Act of 2010, S.3217.

management of their firms while navigating through these troubled waters. With newly heightened expectations for directors to perform ethics and compliance oversight, appointing a strong, independent CECO to act on their behalf is an essential starting point. To do anything less is fraught with peril.

APPENDIX D: TWENTY QUESTIONS THAT BOARDS OF DIRECTORS SHOULD ASK ABOUT COMPLIANCE AND ETHICS

A. Context and Landscape

1. What are the elements of the company's C&E program? How does each of the elements comport with the U.S. Federal Sentencing Guidelines or other relevant standards?

2. What is the budget for the C&E program?

B. Role of the Board

3. What board committee oversees the C&E program? How does the board discharge its legal and extralegal obligations for oversight of the C&E program? What is the method and frequency of C&E reporting to the board, and of board contact with the CECO?

4. How will the board obtain and evaluate the appropriate training and information to discharge its C&E responsibility? How often will the board include C&E on its agenda?

C. Structure and Role of the Compliance and Ethics Officer and Function

5. What high-level corporate personnel are responsible for the implementation, operation, and oversight of the C&E program?

6. Who is the company's chief ethics and compliance officer (CECO)? Is she a senior executive with experience, seniority, authority, autonomy, time, and resources sufficient to do the job? Who does the CECO report to, and what measures are in place to protect her ability to discharge the role with sufficient authority and independence? Does the CECO have unfiltered access to the CEO and board?

7. Has the board passed a resolution setting out the express mandate for the CECO and the compliance function? What are the full- and part-time resources in place to support compliance and ethics? Are compliance-related activities assigned across various levels in the organization? Are managers held accountable for meeting these objectives through the performance review process?

D. Program Status and Operation

8. How are the company's compliance and ethics programs structured? Do they cover the company's high priority risks and global operations, including business partners, vendors, subcontractors, and third-party relationships? What policies, procedures, and internal controls are in place to manage high priority risk areas?

9. What has management (both at the top and in the middle ranks of the organization) done — in both words and visible action — to support ethical conduct and legal compliance? Is the CECO involved and consulted on a regular basis by management regarding the culture of the organization, and how this supports ethical conduct and business decisions that comply with all rules and procedures?

10. What is the process for assessing C&E risks in the organization? Has the company developed and prioritized an inventory of C&E risks?

11. Where in the Code of Ethics/Conduct are responsibilities of all managers, employees, and third parties covered? How are those responsibilities communicated within the company?

12. How does the organization support ethical culture? What is the C&E training program for all levels of the company, including board of directors, managers, employees, and third parties?

13. How does the culture of the organization support the raising of concerns? What are the mechanisms for raising confidential whistleblower concerns, without fear of retaliation, to the top of the organization, including investigation and follow-up protocols?

14. What ongoing reporting, monitoring, and audit processes are in place to assess the effectiveness of the C&E program?

15. How does the organization embed ethical leadership and culture throughout its management, e.g., through incentives and linkage to compensation and the performance evaluation processes?

16. What mechanisms does the Company have in place to regularly and systematically review C&E failures and respond appropriately, including remedial action and improvements to the C&E program?

17. How does the company ensure consistent disciplinary action and enforcement of its Code of Ethics/Conduct at all levels, including senior management?

E. Closing Questions for the CECO

18. What support does the C&E function receive from the CEO and senior management team?

19. Has the board had the program evaluated by a qualified independent expert? Has it performed a cultural assessment? How does the company program compare to its peers, and to best practice in the field?

20. What keeps you (the CECO) up at night? Are there any other matters you wish to raise to the attention of the board (or independent board committee)? What other questions should we be asking you?

REFERENCES

Boehme, Donna C., "From Enron to Madoff: Why Many Corporate Compliance and Ethics Programs Are Doomed to Failure," March 5, 2009, in Michael D. Greenberg, *Perspectives of Chief Ethics and Compliance Officers on the Detection and Prevention of Corporate Misdeeds: What the Policy Community Should Know*, CF-258-RC, Santa Monica, Calif.: RAND Corporation, 2009. As of June 24, 2010: http://www.rand.org/pubs/conf_proceedings/CF258/

———, *Not Your Father's Board Training — What Today's Boards Need to Know About Ethics and Compliance*, archived webinar, EthicsPoint, 2010. As of June 7, 2010: http://www.ethicspoint.com/event/not-your-fathers-board-training---what-todays-boards-need-to-know-about-ethics-and-compliance

Bonime-Blanc, Andrea, and Jacqueline E. Brevard, *Ethics and the Board: Integrating Integrity into Business Strategy*, CP-013, The Conference Board, 2009. As of June 7, 2010: http://www.conference-board.org/pdf_free/councils/TCBCP013.pdf

Brune, C., "Boards Fall Short on Ethics Issues — Update — Survey by the Conference Board," *Internal Auditor*, August 2003. As of June 7, 2010: http://findarticles.com/p/articles/mi_m4153/is_4_60/ai_106863362/

Ethics Resource Center, *Leading Corporate Integrity: Defining the Role of the Chief Ethics and Compliance Officer (CECO)*, Washington, D.C.: Ethics Resource Center, 2007. As of June 7, 2010: http://www.ethics.org/files/u5/CECO_Paper_UPDATED.pdf

Greenberg, Michael D., *Perspectives of Chief Ethics and Compliance Officers on the Detection and Prevention of Corporate Misdeeds: What the Policy Community Should Know*, CF-258-RC, Santa Monica, Calif.: RAND Corporation, 2009. As of June 15, 2010: http://www.rand.org/pubs/conf_proceedings/CF258/

Hurt, Harry III, "Taking Away Directors' Rubber Stamps," *New York Times*, January 17, 2010, p. BU5. As of June 7, 2010: http://www.nytimes.com/2010/01/17/business/17shelf.html

In Re Caremark International Inc. Derivative Litigation, 698 A.2d 959 (Del. Ch. 1996).

Lorsch, Jay, and Jack Young, "Pawns or Potentates: The Reality of America's Corporate Boards," *The Executive*, Vol. 4, No. 4, 1990, pp. 85–87.

Murphy, Joe, "What Government Can Do to Help Prevent Corporate Crime," March 5, 2009, in Michael D. Greenberg, *Perspectives of Chief Ethics and Compliance Officers on the Detection and Prevention of Corporate Misdeeds: What the Policy Community Should Know*, CF-258-RC, Santa Monica, Calif.: RAND Corporation, 2009. As of June 24, 2010: http://www.rand.org/pubs/conf_proceedings/CF258/

National Association of Corporate Directors, *Report of the NACD Blue Ribbon Commission on Risk Governance: Balancing Risk and Reward*, ISBN No. 978-0-943176-45-1, 2009.

Policy and Impact Committee of the Committee for Economic Development, *Restoring Trust in Corporate Governance: The Six Essential Tasks of Boards of Directors and Business Leaders*, Committee for Economic

Development, 2010. As of June 7, 2010: http://www.ced.org/images/library/reports/corporate_governance/cgPolicyBrief0110.pdf

Public Law 107-204, Sarbanes-Oxley Act of 2002, July 30, 2002. As of June 16, 2010: http://frwebgate.access.gpo.gov/cgi-bin/getdoc.cgi?dbname=107_cong_bills&docid=f:h3763enr.tst.pdf

Stone v. Ritter, 911 A.2d 362 (Del. 2006).

U.S. Sentencing Commission, *Amendments to the Sentencing Guidelines*, 2010. As of June 30, 2010: http://www.ussc.gov/2010guid/finalamend10.pdf

Welch, Jack, and Suzy Welch, "How Much Blame Do Boards Deserve?" *Bloomberg Businessweek*, January 14, 2009. As of June 7, 2010: http://www.businessweek.com/magazine/content/09_04/b4117102356265.htm